LIVING WITH THE PASSIVE-AGGRESSIVE MAN

COPING WITH THE PERSONALITY
SYNDROME OF HIDDEN AGGRESSION—
FROM THE BEDROOM TO THE BOARDROOM

Scott Wetzler, Ph.D.

A Fireside Book
PUBLISHED BY SIMON & SCHUSTER
NEW YORK   LONDON   TORONTO   SYDNEY   TOKYO   SINGAPORE

FIRESIDE
Rockefeller Center
1230 Avenue of the Americas
New York, New York 10020

First Fireside Edition 1993
FIRESIDE and colophon are registered trademarks
of Simon & Schuster Inc.

Designed by Irving Perkins Associates
Manufactured in the United States of America

10   9   8   7

Library of Congress Cataloging-in-Publication Data

Wetzler, Scott, date.
    Living with the passive-aggressive man: coping with the personality
syndrome of hidden aggression—from the bedroom to the boardroom /
Scott Wetzler.
        p.   cm.
    Includes index.
    1. Men—United States—Psychology.   2. Passive–aggressive
personality—United States.   3. Man-woman relations—United States.
I. Title.
HQ1090.3.W48   1992
155.3'32—dc20   92-14598
                                                                      CIP

ISBN 0-671-76791-7
ISBN 0-671-87074-2 (pbk.)

While the case studies described in this book are based on interviews
with real persons, the names, professions, locations and other biographi-
cal details about the participants have been changed to preserve their
privacy and anonymity.

To the memory of my father, Benjamin Wetzler

ACKNOWLEDGMENTS

A novice to the world of publishing, I have been extremely fortunate to be shepherded through the process by three talented professionals: Connie de Swaan, whose skillful use of language made the manuscript eminently more readable; Gail Winston of Simon & Schuster, whose editorial advice kept the book true to our initial vision; and Pam Bernstein of the William Morris Agency, who has consistently advocated on my behalf. I am indebted to all of you. In addition, Liz Perle deserves acknowledgment, as she was the first person to recognize the potential of a book on passive-aggressive men.

Several friends are worthy of special mention. My jogging partner, Tom Teicholz, served as a sounding board for all my ideas, read and reread countless drafts, and supported me with his usual good humor, creativity, and insights. David Richenthal, my attorney, was always available to help bring the project to fruition in any and every way. And Dr. Willard Gaylin, mentor and role model, whose intellect is surpassed by his compassion. I thank each one of you.

I am particularly grateful to Dr. Herman van Praag and the Department of Psychiatry at the Albert Einstein College of Medicine/Montefiore Medical Center, which has been my second home for many years, for giving me the time and intellectual stimulation to put my ideas down on paper.

I would like to express my appreciation to the many anonymous patients whose stories are told throughout this book.

And finally, to my wife, Graciela, I am fortunate to offer her my ever-increasing love and devotion.

CONTENTS

INTRODUCTION

As a practicing psychologist, many of the stories I hear women recount about certain men in their lives are strongly similar in detail. This is true whether they are talking about dating, marriage, family conflicts, dynamics on the job or superficial everyday encounters.

A number of patterns tend to pop up in their descriptions of relationships with boyfriends, husbands, fathers or bosses: many of these men unnerve them through convoluted power games, obstructive tactics and lopsided logic. There always seems to be a struggle involved, whether it is about intimacy, respect, success at work or even something as simple as ordering a meal from a waiter. "If I let the guy know what I want," women patients have told me again and again, "then he just makes it *harder* for me to get."

The frustrating and maddening behavior they are talking about actually has a method to it, and a name: *passive-aggression*—and passive-aggressive behavior is what drives these women "crazy." What exactly are the men in their lives doing? How does passive-aggressive behavior play itself out? See if the following real-life incidents appear familiar to you.

—Mark and Heather have been living together for a year, but lately Mark has been playing the "accidental" lover too often. He'll take his clothes off and lie back, giving Heather a look that indicates he wants sex. But she's never quite sure; Mark will neither resist her advances nor show much enthusiasm. Even while having sex, Heather's not sure if he cares about pleasing either one of them, or of being intimate. Ask him what he wants and he'll say, "*You know. . . .*" Ask Mark if he was satisfied, and he may answer by turning away from Heather, garbling a comment, stopping her dead from asking again, or countering with a remark such as, "You always need compliments. . . ."

Afterglow turns into aftershock.

—Jack, a vice president of marketing and a fairly popular man with some good ideas as well as higher aspirations, has been assigned to work with Nora, a colleague in an equal position. Jack prides himself on being "the nerve center" of his department, always telling clients and underlings that he runs things. But this is a belief he alone holds. Nora, a more taciturn personality, has become the driving force behind the success of the department since she arrived at the agency four months ago, a fact Jack cannot deal with.

Now that Jack and Nora must work together on a project for a major client, Nora discovers "who's in charge": Jack neglects to give Nora some crucial phone messages; he makes appointments with the client without informing her; he spends most of his day trying to undermine Nora's progress in getting a deal done with the client. Angry and frustrated, Nora takes Jack out for a drink and confronts him. Jack tells her that "no one is more of a team player than me." The next morning, Jack complains to their boss that Nora is procrastinating in getting the deal done, that she misses appointments with the client, that they're unhappy with her work and that she doesn't return their phone calls.

—Janet has promised her retired parents to make a family dinner, since they rarely see each other except for major holidays. Eddie, her older brother, works long hours at a city newspaper; Janet runs her own mail-order business and has the added responsibility of being a single parent to her twin sons, so it's been difficult to coordinate a good time for all of them.

Finally, Eddie agrees to a time and promises to make himself available. Janet plans a catered dinner and spends a lot of time and money getting it right. Eddie carries on about how he can't wait to see the family, and that of course he'll be at Janet's apartment by seven o'clock, seven-thirty the latest. He calls at six to say he'll be a half hour late—but it's five hours later when he turns up, with no apology.

Janet blows up; their mother begins crying; their father makes accusations about Eddie being "spoiled and selfish." Eddie doesn't understand why everyone is so angry—*he just doesn't get it.*

Eddie said he'd gotten a call about covering what could be a front-page scandal for the paper and went off to meet a source. He thought his family should be happy for him, since it could mean a turning point in his career. Why can't they get off his back? What was one catered dinner compared to his *success*—and besides, *he hadn't asked Janet to cater the damn thing, had he*? He said that they were making a mountain out of a molehill, and why did they always demand things of him exactly when he was off "doing my thing."

What's really happening in these stories? Simply, one person is pushing another person around, but he's doing it *passive-aggressively.* A guy suggests intimacy or makes a promise; you want to believe he's for real; then he reneges and self-righteously turns your grievance aside . . . *and* inside out, accusing *you* of having a problem!

If these sketches strike a chord in you, you've known passive-aggressive behavior. And like Heather, Nora or Janet, you have a right to be angry. Passive-aggressive men don't play fair. A Mark, a Jack or an Eddie may respect, be fond of or even passionately love the women in their lives, *but the women don't know it.*

In relationships, these passive-aggressive men deny a woman's needs and feelings. They close off opportunities to address issues, and they focus on how they can get their own way. Therein lies the dilemma: it seems futile to confront them and infuriating to accept their behavior.

As you go through this book chapter by chapter, you will meet the passive-aggressive man in many forms. He could be a love-obsessed social climber who reinvents his history as he needs it, like *The Great Gatsby*, F. Scott Fitzgerald's quintessential self-creator; a blustering cab driver who ignores your directions to get you home the fastest way, gets lost and angrily complains to you about having to drive a cab; or a ruthless middle manager on his way up a Fortune 500 company. Whoever he is, he can create great turmoil in your life.

PASSIVE-AGGRESSIVE MEN TODAY

The term "passive-aggressive" was first coined during World War II by an Army psychiatrist, Colonel William Menninger, who had been trained to deal with strong negative reactions to military life. Menninger recognized that the military is structured for uniformity and compliance, where individual choice, opinion or expertise does not change the rules, where you are obliged to suspend the determination of your own destiny. He noticed that while men thrived under this rigorous institutional structure, others perished and protested—if not through the craziness that is associated with the hero of *Catch-22*, who tries to get out of the Army on a Section 8, then through benign disobedience. To deal with enforced change and cope with the lack of opportunity for personal choice, these soldiers resisted, ignored orders, withdrew or simply wanted to flee. Menninger labeled this resistance "passive-aggression" and described it as "an immaturity reaction."

Institutions that offer few avenues for individual self-expression, like the military or large bureaucracies, are breeding grounds for passive-aggression, which may be considered a (typically futile) attempt by the weak to thwart the authority of a more powerful opponent. When someone lacks the power and resources to challenge authority directly, the resistance comes out indirectly and covertly.

In a sense the insubordinate soldier of World War II is the prototype of today's passive-aggressive man, who also refuses to do what's expected of him. Passive-aggression has become a widespread problem in our daily lives, going well beyond the military and into personal relationships: at home, in the bedroom, and in the workplace. What makes it a compelling contemporary issue is that it is no longer the story of the weak versus the powerful. It is the story of someone who *thinks* of himself as weak and powerless, and sees passive-aggression as his only response to people whom he *views* as more powerful. His wife is transformed in his mind into a master sergeant, and his boss into a dictator.

The tragedy of passive-aggression today is that the passive-aggressive man *misconstrues* personal relationships as being struggles for power, and sees himself as powerless. And, as you will learn in reading this book, the secret of dealing with a passive-aggressive man is to correct this misperception, and help him to feel more empowered.

Passive-aggression is now so worldwide in scope that passive-aggressive men easily cross boundaries, literally and figuratively. So just as there are men like Mark and Eddie affecting your personal life, so there are high-powered autocrats upsetting the world and its economies—and doing it passive-aggressively. Saddam Hussein, storming into Kuwait, claiming Iraq was the victim of American aggression, taunted us and tested the limits of our patience. He took passive-aggression to a despicable and vicious extreme.

What's far more typical is the candy-coated passive-aggressive who in the night fires his own emotionally packed SCUD missiles in your direction, asking for a fight while blaming you for being in the line of fire. It's what I call the "cold wars" of everyday life.

Not only do I listen to "war" stories from patients about the men they love, live or work with, but I read about openly passive-aggressive acts in the press, relating to politics or business, stories that intrigue me about manipulative men who negotiate the boardroom and bedroom with equal effectiveness. It seems to me that passive-aggression is not only here to stay as a method of relating, but it has become more tolerated and accepted.

What accounts for the apparent increase in passive-aggression, and where did it come from?

Passive-aggression long predates World War II and contemporary American culture, but part of its widespread growth may be related to the revolution in sex roles that has occurred over the last few decades. Thirty years ago, men asserted their machismo by confrontation. If a man wanted something, and fought for it—this was called aggression, and it was sanctioned by society. The art of diplomacy, the use of tact, the role of mediator who smoothed the rough edges and defused serious conflict was a kind of passivity more characteristic of the traditional feminine role.

Prior to the Women's Movement, a dissatisfied wife who was financially dependent on her husband would find it hard to express herself and make demands. Today, as the imbalance of power in relationships has been somewhat redressed, and with greater opportunities for independence, she is more than willing to speak up for herself. As she claimed greater power, some of the men she came into contact with began to feel less powerful, intimidated. Not only did the Women's Movement help women understand assertion, self-respect and actualization of goals in and outside the home, it changed men— some by barely noticeable degrees, others, enormously. Out of the Movement grew the New Woman, but with her, the New Man.

This New Man is given the opportunity to express feelings, cry, allow himself to take some of the financial burdens off his back by agreeing that his spouse/housemate should work if she so chooses, reject some of the stereotyped sex-role designations, help deliver his child and treat women like equals. The Women's Movement created a tidal wave of identity crises, male and female; women want the opportunities men always had open to them, and push for them; men want what they always had—the power—but they give it up or do not give it up, passive-aggressively. Macho isn't dead, just a bit comatose.

For the New Man, it is accepted practice to complain on the job (once thought to be "sissified"), bemoan one's fate, plead poverty and show weakness, rather than always be the old-style stoic, take-a-stand-type leader. In *Power! How to Get It, How to Use It*, Michael Korda writes that some men have turned humiliation into a "productive and profitable system." Whereas at one time men would show pride, authority and direction without thinking twice, life is not the same, and ". . . hence the difficulty in finding anyone who will admit to being responsible for an unpleasant decision—unlike the old days when young men regarded each unpleasant decision as a way station on the road to success, and wanted nothing more than to prove they had made it for themselves, unilaterally, rather than by committee."

Considering the changes wrought by the New Man in his personal and professional lives, I sometimes wonder if the accusatory label "passive-aggressive," which is so freely bandied about, doesn't in fact reveal a certain nostalgia for the 1960s and before, when men were men and you, and they, knew where they stood.

Of course, passive-aggression isn't the exclusive domain of men; women also adopt it. The reason I focus solely on male psychology in this book is that men are passive-aggressive in especially destructive and clumsy ways, upsetting or ruining love and work relationships—or world order. They torment themselves and you. For whatever reason—perhaps because women are socialized differently, learning charm and diplomacy at an early age, or because women have less testosterone—passive-aggression does not represent as serious a psychological problem or conflict for women as it does for men today.

WHY WRITE A BOOK ABOUT PASSIVE-AGGRESSION?

The answer is simple: *passive-aggressive behavior fractures relationships that would otherwise thrive.*

If you've known Mark or Jack or Eddie, the men cited in the previous pages—he's your husband, lover, brother, boss, friend, co-worker—you've seen how he destroys relationships; you've watched as he squanders his potential. And you, too, have probably been deeply affected by this virtuoso of avoidance. You give him a wide berth, and then he mows you down.

This book is for women like you, who deal with, live with, have been hurt by and *have hope for* this unique character: the passive-aggressive man. If you love such a man, then you know him as someone who never seems to love you back fully; he promises but rarely delivers. He sees himself as a casualty of recurrent misunderstandings, a bundle of intricately overlapping layers of behaviors no one can penetrate. What makes his personality confusing is that he's passive, coaxing, elusive, but also aggressively resistant to you, to intimacy, to responsibility and reason.

Right now, confused by his behavior, you may be doubting yourself, not him. If you are involved with a passive-aggressive man, *defining* him can feel as imposing a task as scaling Mount Everest. As an experienced psychologist, I have found that the passive-aggressive man doesn't have the advantage over you here—he is probably as confused about who he is and what makes him tick as you are! But passive-aggression is an understandable psychological pattern—anger its driving force, and fear its hidden secret. As you read this book and recognize the pattern, you will be less confused by the passive-aggressive men in your life and the games they play. The ultimate success or failure of your relationship will be how the two of you willingly deal with his—and your—problems.

As you gain some perspective on the passive-aggressive personality, you can laugh about his games and loop-the-loop logic. You can take him or leave him, and decide what's best for yourself. You've got the ability to call him on his tactics and cut your losses. However, if you're *caught* in the loop—at home, at work or even casually enough to affect your life in some minor way—you may be too emotionally bruised by him to be amused.

When you're "hooked" on a passive-aggressive man (or if you've grown up with one), you've been hurt and made angry by his games far too often. You wish you could take him or leave him, but you don't know why you can't. On one side, there's the passive-aggressive man and his tricks, but on the other side, there's your weakness for him.

In writing this book, I hope to guide you through the labyrinth of passive-aggressive reasoning and behavior, clear up mysteries about his personality and help you pursue issues that cause problems.

My goals for this book are threefold:

(1) To uncover how the passive-aggressive man thinks, feels and acts, and how he got to be that way
(2) To explain why *you* feel the way you do about this man
(3) And finally, to help give you perspective on your relationships with passive-aggressive men; to urge you to examine your expectations and to offer strategies to start healing problem partnerships

This book relates the combined experiences of my patients—described in unrecognizable composites—friends and social observers who have been where you are now. It is not simply an analysis of deviant behavior but an excursion into what women, and passive-aggressive men themselves, do to master the problems and, if possible, change this behavior.

In the upcoming chapters, you'll learn what makes this

behavior as interesting as it is frustrating. Using actual por-
traits of passive-aggressive men, I'll examine up close the
evolution of this man's behavior—*why* and *how* he is who
he is. I'll describe his predominant qualities—the exact games
and behaviors that set traps for him and for you.

I hope that you will come away from this book with valuable insights about how to build relationships, and about
what you want from them. This book will guide you in knowing when to confront a passive-aggressive man, and deciding
for yourself what's best for you. Improved communication
will clarify whether you *can* resolve a problematic relationship, or whether you need to open up your choices and al-
ternatives, and gain the respect you deserve.

We all seek meaning to our emotions and actions—and going
on a journey that will open paths into why we are the way
we are and why we love those we love is a journey worth
taking. I believe in the fundamental gifts we're all given, of
awareness, reason, and the versatile ability to help ourselves
and others. Versatility allows for that *willingness* in all of us
to change what is no longer working in relationships. Change
isn't easy—and trying to change another without his consent
is practically impossible.

What *Living with the Passive-Aggressive Man* offers you
is behavioral information and strategies for changing relationships, with perspectives and experiences of women who
have lived with and loved passive-aggressive men. Primarily,
this book offers you—through understanding and rediscov-
ery—the chance for a new beginning.

1

ANATOMY OF PASSIVE-AGGRESSION

WHEN THE KING of Hearts in *Alice in Wonderland* tries to calm the Mad Hatter's hysteria by saying, "don't be nervous or I'll have you executed on the spot," the warning could easily have emerged from the lips of a passive-aggressive man. "Yes, no!" "Stop, go!" "I never lie, I was just protecting you from the truth!" *What does he mean?* The King of Hearts and most passive-aggressive men share the maddening characteristic of never saying exactly what they mean.

He may be a legal wizard, a computer genius, a brilliant analytical scientist or a guy who runs a newsstand, but when it comes to relating to others, the passive-aggressive man has just learned to read. *He's* as unclear about why he does what he does as you are about his behavior.

When patients describe his psychological abuse, they often begin the same way: "This guy is *impossible*." "This guy is *difficult*." "Every meal, every conversation and everything we decide to do is handled like we're two warring nations negotiating a pact, not two people who care about each other," one woman told me. She could be talking for other women about their husbands, fathers, bosses, the shoemaker.

What's the appeal of a guy who says in one breath, "I love

you/I hate you," or, "I promise . . . /Why should I do anything for you?" If you have any emotional investment in a passive-aggressive man, it's because you've probably fallen for his salesmanship. He's brilliantly persuasive at selling himself—whether it's his brooding stoicism, his understated charm, his boyishness or irresistible seductiveness. You buy into his elusiveness; but you also buy into his *neediness*. You feel for him and want to be the one who breaks through, who tears the walls down and gets him to shape up. In many cases, it is a thankless mission.

Problems arise with the passive-aggressive man because of his fatal flaw: an indirect and inappropriate way of expressing hostility hidden under the guise of innocence, generosity or passivity. If what he says or does confuses you, or, more likely, angers you, this is why. You're not the only one to react this way. It's what passive-aggression is all about.

INSIDE PASSIVE-AGGRESSION

A seemingly paradoxical term, passive-aggression asks the question, How can a person be passive *and* aggressive, rather than one way or the other? It's a common misconception about passive-aggression that its perpetrators swing alternately between the two behaviors—either willfully with premeditation to control others (aggression) or in a self-effacing manner (passivity).

The truth is that the passive-aggressive man doesn't ride an emotional seesaw (although he may put you on one); he's not passive today and aggressive tomorrow, depending on the circumstances. Rather, the passive-aggressive man is simultaneously passive and aggressive. The paradox reigns because he *renounces his aggression as it is happening*.

Since passivity and aggression are contradictory by origin and act, you can see that we are dealing with a complex and fundamentally ambivalent creature.

Passive-aggressive tactics aren't that easily read at first; it takes a while to figure out what this guy is getting at: the blur of meaning lies in his genius for creating discrepancies between how he pretends to be and how he acts, which is a better indicator of his true intentions and feelings. You're always receiving mixed messages because he wants you to guess what he wants almost as much as he wants to fool you or string you along. This is what his double-speak can sound like:

—"I can't live without you," a passive-aggressive boyfriend says as he kisses you and leaves the room. Or, when the two of you are alone, he asks "Why are you around all the time?" when he means, *I'm terrified that you'll leave me.*

—"Are you interested . . . ?" a passive-aggressive husband may whisper to a wife who makes an affectionate advance toward him, while what he is really thinking is, *Why am I asking her when I'm not that turned on?* Or he says, contrarily, "Sometimes sex is overrated," when he means, *I want you,* all the while expecting his wife to know that he wants to be seduced.

—"We've noticed your administrative skills and would like to discuss a special project that's coming up," a passive-aggressive boss says flatteringly, hinting at a promotion, but then you never hear from him again. What he really meant was: *What makes you think I'd even consider you for that secret project, and how'd you find out about it anyway?*

Or, he might try a version of this empty promise:

—"Okay, I know I promised to pick up your kitchen stuff at Sue's place, but my car broke down. Maybe tomorrow . . . " a passive-aggressive brother assures you, but he's thinking, *Why do you keep asking me to do anything involving Sue when you know I can't stand the sight of her, and besides, I hate hauling freight in my new car.*

—Or, a passive-aggressive friend says, "I wanted to be the first one to buy you a disk for your new CD player . . . something *really* great, something you'll love—eighteenth-century harpsichord favorites that took me a week to find for you," but what he thinks is, *This should let you know how low-*

brow your taste in music is. Your idea of culture is the Miami Sound Machine.

The man in each of these examples isn't playing diplomat; his baiting behavior isn't *inadvertent*, though he hopes you'll think it is. This is a man who's driven to appear above suspicion, guiltless and guileless. That's why you find that most passive-aggressive men negotiate the world as "nice guys" denying even the slightest hint of hostility or conflict.

As with a brother who'll easily break a promise five or ten times rather than just say, "No, sorry, I can't," this man will lie to keep you on a string until the game reaches its limit and he's finally forced—by you—to confess that he can't come through. If he's someone who's been in your life a long time, you may find you're always arguing about the same thing, year after year. Most of all, you wonder why you still jump through the same flaming hoops he holds up, how he can still get a rise out of you.

If you're typical, and at the end of your rope with him, you may fantasize about ending your relationship—and this includes abandoning relationships with "impossible" relatives, like fathers and brothers. But you don't act on it. Or, if he's a key player sorely affecting your job, you might just give up and quit, but the passive-aggressive colleague you leave behind won't believe he's done anything to obstruct your career. More likely, he expects a huge pat on the back for *doing everything* to boost your efforts and calls you ungrateful, to boot.

Whoever he is, your relationship with a passive-aggressive man probably leaves you feeling unsettled and insecure, wondering why you're always at an emotional crossroad. Most of all, you wonder how to make your life with him a better place to be. Before I get to the latter, I'll take you through what makes him tick and keeps him running. The passive-aggressive man's *modus operandi* has two primary component parts: passivity and aggression. Let's begin there.

A CLOSE LOOK AT PASSIVITY

When it's used as a power play against you, *passivity* can rouse you to anger just as much as an active display of hostility. But why does someone's *in*action so anger you?

The answer lies in the qualities that make up "passivity." Traditionally, a passive person shows little initiative in getting what he wants; assertion is a labor and comes about hesitantly, if at all. Male passivity covers a wide range of behavior, from the classic "loser"—the weak, inept type who has a hard time keeping a job—to the "conformist"—the man who rolls with the current, buoyed by approval seeking, not making waves, changing his opinions in order to be liked and rarely stating what he feels and thinks at any moment.

In certain corporate or bureaucratic circles, he's the yes-man. On occasion, his quick-change sentiments delivered to the right person at the right time may serve to get him what he wants. As *a guy who just wants to fit in*, he may reach some level of success, but he's a poor leader and decision maker; he avoids big responsibilities, and he'll stop short of a top spot. As he sees it, others are better able to make the right decisions.

"*This man's a baby*. He's sharp, he's charming, but emotionally, he's about four years old!" women say, and they're right. Passive people—and here I include women, too—all suffer because they haven't quite grown up. They're childlike and continue to rely on others.

Larry is a good example of passive dependency. An engineer in the construction business, he can never remember to bring cash, check, or credit card when he goes out to dinner. It isn't that Larry is cheap; rather, he has a compulsion to get others to pay for his meal—he needs you to feed him. His excuses take the same unrealistic and juvenile line of thinking as, "The dog ate my term paper." You don't believe Larry's story, but it is that boyish, ingratiating look—that need to be loved and forgiven—that suckers certain of us who take to babying him. That Larry needs to be "nurtured" by someone with money—that is, an adult with power—makes him passive; that he has to *trick* you into doing it makes him *passive-aggressive*.

You'll find that passive men and the more complicated passive-aggressive men have a trait in common: both are reluctant to assert themselves directly, in a firm but tactful way. They shun and fear *self-assertion*, mistaking it for unleashed aggression. The consequences of assertion scare them. Their internal line of thinking goes something like this: "If I do this, straight out and simply, I'm telling you what I think, what I'm going to do or what I feel. This leaves me open to a possible challenge, disagreement or loss of support."

This emotion-packed reasoning haunts them: If asserting themselves brings them into direct confrontation with others, what will happen next? Could they handle an attack? Self-doubt tells them they would not be able to, so they do what they can to avoid confrontation, winding and weaving all over the map. To passive and passive-aggressive personalities, denial and avoidance offer a safe haven. This is one reason why the roads in a passive-aggressive man's life lead to detours, dead ends or clover-leaf turns that circle back to the starting point: going *forward* puts him on his bumpiest road.

The passive-aggressive man pretends to be passive, when he's not that way at all. What underlies his apparent passivity—his fear and dependency—is aggression, pure and simple. And this is what rouses you to anger, makes you feel tricked. The passive personality is never infuriating because he poses no challenge; the passive-aggressive personality, however, is constantly giving you little tastes of his hostility in doses just large enough to irritate you.

Aggression is the other side of the issue. While passivity brings out restraint, inhibition, and a life without much challenge or "juice," aggression evokes images of force, energy and push. Together they add up to a mixed-up view of his power as a man.

A CLOSE LOOK AT AGGRESSION

Aggression, a basic drive older than predawn man, is often thought of as man's failing—a dubious impulse equated with hostility, tyranny, anger, dominance and bloodshed. Yet aggression exists within a wide range of experience, and everyone is motivated to some degree by aggressive impulses. A masked terrorist aiming an Uzi at a planeload of tourists is one kind of riotous aggressor; a rude shopper pushing his way to the front of a line in a bakery and demanding to be served reveals another kind of unbridled nerve; pitching a set of dishes at the kitchen wall during a fight is anger with impact; and a Jets quarterback whose guts and muscle win a football game describes aggression a fourth way.

Of the two impulses, it is aggression, not passivity, that commands greater attention by social, psychological, biological, ethical and religious scholars, scientists, researchers and philosophers. Perhaps it is the power and intensity of aggression that fascinates us; it's a force that can build or destroy with equal strokes. Aggression not only makes headlines, it gets things done. Yet, those who study it unanimously view aggression as something to be contained.

The messages from social theorists, for example, reckon that aggression swims the eternal tides of our primordial gene pools—a remnant from the days before we were civilized and prowled the earth as animals. Aggression got us dinner, shelter and mates. It still does, but now it has a civilized veneer. However, some social theorists ask, with developed forebrains and space-age technologies, do we really need such impulses? Aggression, being more destructive than constructive, undoes the fabric of society, and results in war, crime and domestic violence. Theorists say we must control aggression, and we have built jails and a criminal justice system to do it.

Ethical philosophers, concerned only with behavior (action) not thoughts (unacted-upon ideas), inject aggression into a similar vein: to them, it's immoral. Their message is: behave in a hostile manner and you'll be judged harshly and suffer guilt that will follow you through life. Theologians, whose scope reaches to an individual's innermost soul, hold aggression as sinful and goodness as holy. Their message is more damning, full of brimstone and with even less understanding of the nature of man: don't feel anger or you'll go to hell. In quite different ways, each of these theories encourages the development of passive-aggression because they discourage the individual from acknowledging, or acting upon, his anger.

Psychology offers a contrasting message: everyone has aggressive impulses and it is beneficial for the individual's mental health to express them, but we must do so appropriately. If, for example, someone less talented and less experienced than you receives the promotion at work you want, it's not a good idea to show the anger you feel in any way that would sabotage your future possibilities of getting ahead. If you want to find out why you weren't promoted, you'd have to know your boss's style, how to approach him/her, in what manner to get the information you need and to know how much to say about your disappointment at losing out. You could even use your frustration to make yourself work that much harder.

But if you're annoyed because someone just recklessly cut in front of you on a highway, then it may be more appropriate to express yourself by word or gesture. Sometimes there are consequences—maybe the guy tries another move to rear-end you in retaliation but, more likely, he'll respond, too, by word or gesture. This kind of direct and appropriate response is better than quietly seething, doing nothing or taking it out on someone else later on.

What humanity has in common is that we're all aggressive in some way. We also share the capacity to *judge* our aggressive acts, weighing them, comparing them, scrutinizing them, containing them. Were we too pushy, too loud, too demanding, too hostile, too prone to tantrums . . . ?

As long as we're willing to take a look at how we're being aggressive, we can *hope* to control the impulse before it becomes destructive. What makes some people aggressive personalities is how *frequently* and *pervasively* they act on their aggressive impulses, whether it's Ralph Cramden on "The Honeymooners," perpetually exasperated, or "L.A. Law" 's Arnie Becker, a quintessential two-stepping attorney on the offense.

But most important, the man who's more vociferous in his aggression isn't necessarily more *aggressive* than the guy who's more subtle about it. The latter may just be more *passive-aggressive*.

As with other impulses and feelings that are difficult to compare or measure from person to person (the unresolvable argument of who loves more . . . who hates more . . . who hurts more . . .), so is it impossible to determine who's really more aggressive. What matters is the type of aggressive acts and how they're handled. Aggression employed to destroy, such as a husband who "accidentally" incinerates papers you need for work tomorrow, versus aggression used to build, such as fighting for what you believe is right, is more significant than how often the impulse is discharged.

Sigmund Freud and the early psychiatrists believed that if people didn't let off steam gradually, aggressive impulses would mount internally, putting excessive pressure on the fragile psyche. They thought that aggressive impulses, like water fracturing the walls of a dam, would break through and flood the psyche, causing sudden and explosive acts of aggression—wreaking havoc. The popped cork!

Freud's hydraulic metaphor is only a partial truth. Aggression, like love, isn't a limited commodity to be apportioned, spent, or lost. Rather, when aggression is ventilated one way, the desire to keep it going increases. Still, I believe, as did Freud, that aggression and anger require management and, in some cases, conscientious vigilance. Most important, the energy and impulses that govern aggression can be channeled into creative achievements, productive acts, and improved relationships, the most successful ways of handling them.

"Anger is a human emotion . . . " psychologist Carol Tavris wrote in her book *Anger: The Misunderstood Emotion*, "because only people can judge actions for their intention, jus-tifiability and negligence. Each angry episode contains a series of split-second decisions." So the decisions you make may be alternately (1) to bury or cool the anger/aggression: you may run it off, scrub the kitchen, make a piece of sculpture or ingest something "forbidden"—alcohol, a tray of brownies, high-fat fast food—to "reward" yourself and calm down; or (2) to let it all hang out, telling the object of your anger why you feel as you do. However you decide to deal with your anger, it is under your control.

APPROPRIATE PASSIVE-AGGRESSION

Under certain conditions, passive-aggression can be a healthy, highly adaptive response. Call it subtlety, tact, humor, re-straint, altruism or even courage, it is also passive-aggression. Humor or diplomacy, for example, can defuse a highly vol-atile situation and prevent the dropping of bombs, real or metaphorical. More dramatic cases of passive-aggression are the "nonviolent" protests led by Mahatma Gandhi and Mar-tin Luther King, Jr.

For anyone who is oppressed, truly deprived of power and with no other means of resistance, nonviolent protest is one way to get feelings and demands known: the lone Chinese student stalwartly defying a tank moving on him in Tian-anmen Square is now a universal symbol of such defiance. To assert oneself, without showing inflammatory anger, is, in this case, healthy.

There is a clear distinction between healthy and neuroti-cally played-out passive-aggression. It's the difference be-tween tact and avoidance, humor and obnoxiousness, civil disobedience and plain obstructionism. You know it when you see it in action. A healthy person uses passive-aggression to help him achieve his goals. *Neurotic* passive-aggression clouds issues and gets you nowhere.

To some degree, passive-aggression describes *everyone*, normal as well as dysfunctional men and women. Its universality may be compared to a commonly understood feeling like *anxiety*. It may be an unpleasant emotion, but anxiety serves a psychological function necessary for survival: it signals us to take action when faced with impending danger, motivating us, hopefully, to perform at our best to get us out of the scrape and to a better state.

Evolution has its reasons. Maintaining a moderate level of anxiety is one of our most important adaptive functions. Too much anxiety interferes with functioning—you just freeze or flail—and too little provides insufficient incentive to take action. Similarly, the issue with passive-aggression is not that the behavior is present, but that *what is there is excessive or inappropriate*. When it pervades all different kinds of interactions, not just isolated instances, passive-aggression becomes neurotic.

It's this inappropriateness that causes all the trouble.

IDENTIFYING THE PASSIVE-AGGRESSIVE MAN

A man who's passive-aggressive can function, make plans, make love, win career battles. He may even take up residence in the White House, as did Richard Nixon, a classic profile of this personality type. He revealed himself as an insightful foreign-affairs strategist and an impressive figure "one-on-one," but when he was hurt by public criticism, he felt victimized and betrayed, put upon and sacrificing, often stressing his credentials, as if they would excuse his actions ("I am the President").

Considered brilliant and competitive, Nixon was equally tormented by his jealousies, especially of men born into advantage. Much of politics relies on subterfuge or diplomacy, "counterintelligence," outsmarting the enemy and never letting others know too much of your plans and motives. It's the perfect profession for a passive-aggressive man. However, it was Nixon's profound sense of inadequacy, a real lack of self-respect, that led to his downfall.

This lack of self-esteem is shared by all passive-aggressive men.

Passive-aggressive men are rarely "bad guys," brutalizers, tyrants at home or at work, Lotharios or anti-social con men. But they're not purely "good guys" either, and all that implies—an updated version of "Mr. Right," tolerably flawed but otherwise "perfect." Instead, they're the men who frustrate you—men who suffer from subtle and profound internal bluffs, mechanisms destined to trip up both of you.

They can be great squanderers of time, talent and feelings, making you feel alternately sabotaged and hurt, manipulated and used, undermined and betrayed, devalued and patronized. One moment you're sure of them, the next they're withholding and cold. While you try ardently to get a job done or keep a relationship working, you wind up wasting your time in a dead-end situation.

Above all, the passive-aggressive man is riddled with conflicts, contradictions and convoluted layers of "truths" by which he is guided and to which he clings. Look closely and you'll see an angry man, who is *afraid* of his anger, simmering in resentment and brooding fear, all hiding behind a facade of congeniality. "Mr. Nice Guy" is pure camouflage. He's a commando in self-protection, trudging through miles of effluvia of underlying hostility. Expect to be spattered.

Let's see what kicks up the dirt.

Other psychological syndromes, such as depression, are more precise in their patterns and causes and effects, but passive-aggressive behavior doesn't fit neatly into any absolute boundaries. Although passive-aggression is fundamentally about one individual's psychological conflict, it is most poignantly played out in the arena of a two-person relationship. The passive-aggressive man needs an adversary—*you*—to be the object of his hostility. He also needs someone whose demands and expectations he can resist. Passive-aggression is often expressed through relationships and so appears to be a "relationship" problem. But more often than not, it is one person's problem: *his*.

Wendy's story is a great example of this behavior. When she came to see me for treatment, her focus was the state of her relationship with Vic, a divorced stockbroker. Her overall grievance was Vic's neglectfulness. As Wendy related the mounting and significant number of Vic's "little" omissions, I could see why this relationship was a fragmented one. Wendy described what happened:

> Vic would sometimes "forget" that we had a date and at other times he would appear at my house without calling first. He wanted me to be happy that he'd come over—and I was— but I knew that what also made Vic happy was that he'd caught me off guard.
>
> Then he'd be so sweet that I'd feel I was being unfair. The next day, he'd behave as if we'd just met! He'd be distant and irritated. If I asked what was wrong, he'd shout me down so I couldn't get a straight answer. If I told him he hurt my feelings, he'd say, "I can't help it if you're easily insulted."
>
> I'm losing sleep over this guy, but I can't seem to get closer to him or to break it off either.

What makes Wendy's experience important in the overall analysis is that these "little" interactions with Vic are instantly recognizable to a woman involved with a guy like Vic. You probably understand why Wendy is angry, why she is *entitled* to her anger, why she might be blaming herself and why she has sought help. Vic, however, shows little consideration for her feelings, her standards or her time. Yet, because Wendy cares about him, she accommodates herself to his demands. She doubts herself but believes in him.

Let's analyze things between them a bit more deeply: Wendy loves Vic and she wants him to love her back, but she finds she's more occupied with unraveling his mind's workings than developing real intimacy with him. How he thinks and how he behaves are so alien to Wendy that they fascinate and frustrate her at the same time. *What is he up to now?* Vic's not perfect, but there is enough about him that keeps her interested and emotionally attached to him. If only, she thinks, there weren't so many *games* being played.

What bothers Wendy most is that Vic hides behind a veil of innocence and good intentions, dodging responsibility while belligerently insisting that he's pulling his weight. He puts a spin on her legitimate complaints about him so *he* comes out the wronged party. And she's not sure what she's done to offend him. There's aggression in the acts men like Vic commit, but it's not open warfare—it's more like back-handed hostility.

When it finally became clear to Wendy through therapy that Vic was the prototypical passive-aggressive man, she no longer blamed herself or doubted her reactions. Her antagonist had a name—the passive-aggressive man—and, although the knowledge did not instantly cure her wounded feelings, she could begin dealing with him by *knowing* what drove him.

What will identifying the Vics in your life do for you? Like Wendy, you can clarify the ambiguity inherent in your relationship with such men. Passive-aggression causes emotional confusion and pain. The identifying—or labeling—process will differentiate your problems from his. You needn't feel like a failure because your efforts to communicate with him are ineffective. It's not your fault, and you're not the only one who feels this way. The identifying process should give you perspective on the relationship and help you formulate healthier responses to his machinations.

The complexity and ambiguity of the passive-aggressive man's behavior can make recognizing him—at first—a difficult but not impossible task. *Identification* is the first step toward dealing effectively with him.

THE PASSIVE-AGGRESSIVE PROFILE

The passive-aggressive man may pretend to be sweet or compliant, but beneath his superficial demeanor lies a different core. He's angry, petty, envious, and selfish. He's often not as good as he pretends to be, but neither is he as bad as he feels he is. How do we reconcile these "irreconcilable opposites"?

Understanding the cause of a person's behavior does not excuse it. The person who serves food in a soup kitchen several nights a week after work only to "make up for evil thoughts" is no less admirable for doing it. Similarly, the fact that the passive-aggressive man's behavior is motivated by psychological dynamics, such as anger, dependency, fear of autonomy or power, *doesn't* make him any less responsible for his actions.

Understanding passive-aggression doesn't make hurtful behavior any more tolerable. If a passive-aggressive man treats you badly, then it matters little why he does it. However, by writing this book, I hope to help you resolve the problems of living or working with him and to understand the psychology behind his game. The better you know him, the less likely you are to be threatened or victimized by him.

You'll find that the following traits pretty much describe the range of passive-aggressive behavior. A passive-aggressive man won't have every single one of these traits, but he'll have many of them. By the same token, these traits don't make up the man's *whole* personality. He may have other traits as well, which are not passive-aggressive.

As we go along, I'll guide you through the steps in learning how to cope with a passive-aggressive man—containing him, confronting him and accepting him—and if he is willing to help himself, helping him change. But first, what to look for?

—*Fear of dependency.* Unsure of his autonomy and afraid of being alone, he fights his dependency needs—usually by trying to control you. He wants you to think he doesn't depend on you, but he binds himself closer than he cares to admit. Relationships can become battlegrounds, where he can only claim victory if he denies his need for your support.

—*Fear of intimacy.* Guarded and often mistrustful, the passive-aggressive man is reluctant to show his emotional fragility. He's often out of touch with his feelings, reflexively denying feelings he thinks will "trap" or reveal him, like love. He picks fights just to create distance between you.

—*Fear of competition*. Feeling inadequate, he is unable to compete with other men in work and love. He may operate either as a self-sabotaging wimp with a pattern of failure, or he'll be the tyrant, setting himself up as unassailable and perfect, needing to eliminate any threat to his power—male or female. Few passive-aggressive men are "good sports."

—*Obstructionism*. Just tell the passive-aggressive man what you want, no matter how small, and he may promise to get it for you. But he won't say when, and he'll do it deliberately slowly just to frustrate you. Maybe he won't comply at all. He blocks any real progress he sees to your getting your way.

—*Fostering chaos*. The passive-aggressive man prefers to leave the puzzle incomplete, the job undone, taking on more and more responsibilities until his life is nothing but unfinished business. He sets up ongoing chaotic situations that are intolerable if your life is linked to his. But should you offer a useful suggestion to improve things, just watch his resentment grow.

—*Feeling victimized*. The passive-aggressive man protests that others unfairly accuse him rather than owning up to his own misdeeds. To remain above reproach, he sets himself up as the apparently hapless, innocent victim of your excessive demands and tirades.

—*Making excuses and lying*. The passive-aggressive man reaches as far as he can to fabricate excuses for not getting to a meeting on time, making love, meeting deadlines, fulfilling promises. As a way of withholding information, affirmation or love—to have power over you—the passive-aggressive man may choose to make up a convoluted story rather than give a straight answer. Not only is he a genius at ignoring reality when he so chooses, so he is a virtuoso at spinning tales to make reality look better.

—*Procrastination*. The passive-aggressive man has an odd sense of time—he believes that deadlines don't exist for him.

As he dawdles and procrastinates far beyond most anyone else's limit of patience, opportunities are lost and time is squandered.

—*Chronic lateness and forgetfulness.* One of the most infuriating and inconsiderate of all passive-aggressive traits is this man's inability to arrive on time. By keeping you waiting, he sets the ground rules of the relationship. And his selective forgetting ("Oh, I'm sorry, I forgot to pick up the groceries") is, literally, not to be believed—it's too convenient and self-serving, used only when he wants to avoid an obligation.

—*Ambiguity.* He's the master of mixed messages and sitting on fences, and his language is filled with nonspecific suggestions. He's good at "maybe we can go away for the weekend . . . let's hang loose . . . maybe we can have dinner." When he tells you something, you may still walk away wondering if he actually said yes or no.

—*Sulking.* Feeling put upon when he is unable to live up to his promises or obligations, the passive-aggressive man retreats from pressures around him and sulks, pouts and withdraws. Deep sighs are his preferred mode of communication, which makes reaching him all the more difficult.

As these traits tell us, a passive-aggressive man tries to hide his insecurities and fears by grandstanding. The key to his personality is the fear underlying his aggression. Once you know this, you'll be empowered to act differently and try to change the relationship, or decide to leave.

What I hope to impress upon you in this book is how to recognize and know a passive-aggressive man for what he is, *not for what you wish he could be.* There are many ways of dealing with a passive-aggressive man that can help you minimize the consequences of his behavior on you. In time, you won't fall for the same emotionally torturing games again and again. And, most of all, if he is willing, you'll be able to get the best from him and make your relationship work. Before I continue exploring the intricacies of the passive-aggressive man, let's look at *you,* how he makes you feel and what you can do about it.

2

ON AN EMOTIONAL
SEESAW WITH THE
PASSIVE-AGGRESSIVE MAN

ONE PATIENT'S HUSBAND half painted the window frames in their bedroom, she told me, and has been promising to finish them for two years. When guests ask about the half-gray/half-white frames, Susan tells them by way of explanation, "The phone rang." Over the years, she's managed to defuse her irritation and frustration with humor, but every night she is reminded of what her husband won't complete. It is, she says, "crazy-making."

The unfinished project wrapped in promises is a classic passive-aggressive tactic, and Susan's response is both knowing and compliant. She's learned that asking him to finish the painting doesn't get it done; threatening to do it herself makes him hostile ("It's my business; I keep out of *your* stuff"); and suggesting the name and price of a painter makes him furious ("You really like to take over, don't you?"). Now she's adapted to the situation, in her way. She points out the incomplete job, in his presence, always with a laugh. Bob laughs too, even though he's heard her joke fifty times, but he hasn't yet become reacquainted with the paintbrush.

While the marriage works for her, and Bob is right for her in most ways, Susan, like other women involved with a passive-aggressive man, has moments of self-doubt when she blames herself and believes Bob's charges that she's overbearing, unreasonable and/or demanding.

How is this my fault she asks. *Why is this my problem?*

It's not only the big issues in your relationship with a passive-aggressive man that affect your daily life with him, it's also the little things that mount up: what he forgets and how often; what he denies and stubbornly continues to deny even after you show him the incriminating evidence; what he won't hear, what he won't do, how easily he doesn't give, how casually he lies. As with Susan, there will be certain situations that are bound to irritate you, and others you can live with.

The passive-aggressive man has an uncanny ability to create maddening situations. You want more from him—real emotional connection or a show of cooperation, less edginess and antagonism, less self-consciousness between the two of you. But how can you get it? Is it you or is it him? Are you asking too much of him? When you talk it over, if he agrees with anything, it will be: how you're to blame . . . how you're always wanting more . . . how you never appreciate him . . . how you only see the half-painted window frames, not the bookcase he built . . . how hard he works . . . what sacrifices he makes. For the passive-aggressive man, it's always about you, not him.

From his perspective, these accusations make sense. *If you're to blame, then he's not.* He savors the status quo— and he will try to engineer things so that *you* don't change either. All too often, he gets his way.

As you ride an emotional seesaw with the passive-aggressive man, the important thing to remember is that *it's his problem*. You are not responsible for his passive-aggressive behavior. It's not your fault.

In this chapter I'll look at the key issues of how he makes

you feel, and what you can do about this complicated relationship. These areas are:

1. *How he gets you to doubt yourself.*
   How the passive-aggressive man persuades you that you're the one with a problem; how he jabs at your weak spots while expecting an apology; and how he masterminds and sets up "blurred boundaries."

2. *How you may encourage passive-aggression.*
   Any woman who consistently finds herself involved with passive-aggressive men is likely to wonder (a) *how she chose* a passive-aggressive man in the first place, (b) *why she permits his behavior*, whether he's a relative, husband, boyfriend, boss or colleague and (c) *how she may inadvertently or willfully encourage* his passive-aggression. My aim here is not to put the blame on you, but to help you examine your relationship and make you aware of what's going on from both sides. This is the only way you'll learn. . . .

3. *How to protect yourself.*
   Finally, I'll examine your options, specifically how you can (a) *set limits* to protect yourself and the relationship, thereby making it better, or (b) *choose to get out.*

HOW HE GETS YOU TO DOUBT YOURSELF

The passive-aggressive man is gifted at engineering a sense of doubt in others, and he knows it. He gets you to doubt your impressions of his behavior and to believe *his* version of what's happened. He relies on you to discount your own reactions. No matter how hostile or undermining his passive-aggressiveness, he gets you to make allowances for him, ignore your feelings and take his abuse.

An extreme version of the man who creates knee-weakening doubt and ably shifts blame from himself is the pathological fortune-hunting husband in the film *Gaslight*. Charles Boyer plays the diabolical husband who systematically sets about to convince his young and trusting wife that she's losing her mind. His purpose is to drive her slowly mad until he can find and claim the jewels he knows she's inherited. He counts on succeeding and plans to have his wife put away in a mental hospital so he can take off with the bounty. He uses mind-bending games to undermine his wife's sanity, such as denying he's done or said something. She searches for a brooch she knows she left on the dressing table, but he has already hidden it in the attic, "reminding" her of her memory problem and how she always seems to be losing things. And of course, when the gaslight in the house flickers and she remarks on it, he says, "*What* flickering light?"

In *your* life, the passive-aggressive man's more benign version of "gaslighting" you (telling you that what *is*, *isn't* and vice versa), is just as confusing. At his best, he can provoke an otherwise calm and rational woman into an irrational rage, turning a simple telephone message into a ten-minute routine. It's not necessarily what he says or does, it's how he *obstinately* twists reality and denies the facts to either weasel out of responsibility or push you around. ("You're wrong about our date. I put tomorrow down in my book, not yesterday. That's why I *have* a book. One o'clock is still good for me. But I may have to go out of town. Give me a call if you want to have lunch in a few days.") This is what gets to you.

It's not unusual to develop an especially active temper around him, even become violent for the first time in your life. The maddeningly provocative behavior of passive-aggression has moved women to toss dishes across the room; rip up clothes; build bonfires in the bathtub of his photos, books and letters. If your rage has escalated and you find that you are suddenly shrill or cruel to others, you probably will stop in your tracks and wonder how you've been transformed into this creature of destruction. Ashamed of your behavior, your pattern may be to give in and agree with him that you *are* the persecutory figure he says you are, and he the unfortunate victim. You wind up apologizing to *him*.

A passive-aggressive man plays on your open-mindedness

and willingness to empathize with him. You give that extra inch, then he slaps you in the face with your generosity. This is because there are two realities in operation: what's actually happening between the two of you, and what he wants you to believe.

If he's cool, withdrawn and uncommunicative, he'll give you little signals asking you to sympathize with him or to humor him out of his mood; but if you act on those signals, he's annoyed. He wants you to think you caused his mood but he won't tell you how. The truth is that his cool detachment gets the heat out of his feelings for you so he can withdraw from intimacy. If he says something wounding ("Listen, Dee, my sister doesn't need your advice about handling boys. She's young and attractive. Okay?"), he'll deny his intent and turn the tables on you ("Why are you so sensitive about your age?").

Your better judgment tells you he is being hostile, but you question yourself instead of confronting him. You attribute your reaction to your oversensitivity, not his *in*sensitivity, which he is loathe to discuss. The minute you doubt yourself, the passive-aggressive man seizes the upper hand. His rejoinder is meant to do just that: "Why are you so upset?" or "Relax, you'll live longer."

Provoked by his ploys and entitled to feel angry, you want to lash out at him, but if you do, watch how the tide turns. Did he insult your appearance? Tell him and he'll say, "Can't you take constructive criticism? How many men really notice the details like I do?" Tell a colleague he insulted your intelligence and he'll say, "You took what I said out of context."

Forget about expecting sincere apologies. They're a grace practically unknown to a passive-aggressive man. When offered, they are empty since he claims the harm he's caused was completely inadvertent. But it takes unerring aim to find your weak spot so consistently.

Once you recognize your emotional reaction to such interactions, things begin to make sense. I'm convinced that emotions and intuition are much better indicators than intellect for detecting passive-aggressive maneuvers. The sense of irritation, feeling let down, losing your patience are your best alarms. Obviously, there are times when you *are* hypersensitive or overreact to an offhand remark—times when it *is* your problem. But what you need is a clear and accurate assessment of what happens between you and why you end up feeling lousy with this guy. To stop doubting yourself, become aware of the passive-aggressive man's game and what it's intended to do—put you down.

Women often ask me why they manage to buy into the passive-aggressive man's perspective and doubt themselves. Here's a man, after all, who often won't admit he's wrong, and more often, shows no empathy for you. Why would you blame yourself?

Human sensibility being what it is, when you're on the receiving end of projected anger—and, remember, a passive-aggressive man's game is based on *his* disowned anger—something interesting happens. While you may not have felt angry with him to begin with, once he projects *his* anger onto you ("You've always been such an angry woman. Just get off my back!"), you finally *do* become angry. His manipulative ploy is to focus on your rage, not his ineptitude.

This role reversal is especially common in intense relationships where boundaries between where one person stops and the other begins tend to be less well defined. The fuzzier the dividing line between people, the more they act like a single symbiotic unit rather than two separate individuals and the more they project feelings onto each other. When boundaries become blurred, the details of who felt what first is lost, and what follows is a rewriting of history. This leaves both people confused as to "who's right" and "what happened."

Blurred boundaries are common in healthy relationships— so don't worry if they occur; usually your partner can be trusted. But the passive-aggressive man takes advantage of blurred boundaries to evade responsibility. Projecting feelings, good ones and bad ones, helps people form strong bonds. With the passive-aggressive man, however, these bonds can become shackles.

As boundaries between you fall away, his failures may become your failures. It happens all the time in families, between lovers, even at work, where, with the intensity of a project, you live in each other's pockets. His screw-ups hurt you as much as they hurt him. If you are emotionally distanced from him, it's easier to confront him, call him on his game and/or leave; it's then possible to reestablish boundaries between you and protect yourself. If, however, you're emotionally bound to him, the passive-aggressive man will use his own foibles and feelings as weapons against you.

A passive-aggressive man is not interested in changing himself and alleviating your doubts. If, like Susan (the patient wife in the opening story), you want to keep the relationship going, it will be your job to defuse a passive-aggressive man's negative effect on you and, with new inner strength, change the relationship. Although *changing* is probably the last thing he wants to do, you may be able to break through to him, depending on the strategies you use and how patiently you persist with them.

First of all, *you* must be the one to reset the boundaries. This forms the basis for clear, honest, and open communication. Confront his obvious lies—an accurate sense of shared personal history is a prerequisite for any relationship, business or romantic. Unravel his ambiguities—you need to know where he stands and what you can count on him for. And finally, you need to know how *you* feel, so you can be clear with him. Let him know how far things can go and what is acceptable and unacceptable in how he treats you. This will put you more in control and less likely to be taken advantage of. The section on setting limits, coming up shortly, will help determine the kind of boundaries you need to set and how to do it.

HOW YOU MAY ENCOURAGE PASSIVE-AGGRESSION

In my practice, many patients spend the bulk of their hour complaining about their frustration with the passive-aggressive man they're involved with, saying things like: "He won't cooperate," "He's distant," "He won't even commit to a *time* when we can be together, never mind the day," "Anything he's involved with becomes a juvenile string of power-plays that wind up wasting time and are often beside the point," "He has no respect for me."

When I ask if they might be doing or saying something that encourages his passive-aggressive tactics, they become noticeably uncomfortable, perplexed or defensive. They either draw a total blank, or if my question registers, they can't specifically say how. The question is an important one to answer for yourself if you want to improve your relationship with a passive-aggressive man.

While you probably don't consciously encourage his elusiveness and twisted logic, there's a real dynamic going on between the two of you—remember, without you, his passive-aggression goes nowhere. Somewhere in the relationship, you allow him to be passive-aggressive, if you don't actually encourage it. These are the "terms" that both of you reached—some spoken and some tacit. These terms affect the degree to which passive-aggressive behavior is handled between the two of you.

Patterns of relating may be established during the earliest days of knowing each other, but terms of a relationship aren't chiseled in stone and fixed in concrete. People are flexible—*more than they believe*—and conditions between men and women are more conducive to change than we suspect. Most of all, you are always entitled to renegotiate terms at any point, redefining a relationship until it is mutually acceptable. This means with *any* passive-aggressive man who's part of your life.

If you grow up with a father or brother, or both, who are passive-aggressive, you're pretty much at the mercy of their machinations when you're young. It takes some exposure to the world, experience dealing with other types of men and valuing your own opinion of what's happening before you can confront them and protect yourself. Growing up with passive-aggressive men may unconsciously trip you into encouraging it in other men—as much as you dislike it.

So let's say you've just met a man who interests you. During the honeymoon period, you're more accepting of the man and his quirks, even if he runs hot and cold emotionally, making seductive promises that you belatedly realize he never kept. You notice these lapses, but you're willing to understand. Then you begin to feel the crunch of his heel, especially when his secretary calls to postpone dates for him or when he calls you at one in the morning to casually chat about his day. You start wondering, what does he want from this relationship? He seems interested, yet he's not really *there*. Then you realize you know little or nothing about him; or his stories seem to conflict. Or he avoids intimate revelations that usually come out of a simple information-exchanging conversation.

A patient recently described just such a conversation she had with a passive-aggressive man she'd been dating for a month. Neal was a thirty-six-year-old writer of political speeches who was smart and seductive but incapable of a simple response. Barbara said she never knew how he felt about her at any time. She told me:

Neal asked me how I got into advertising and marketing. I told him that the pace of the business always attracted me, but I didn't know how it worked until I took a course in it. Then, in a sentimental moment, I told him I almost sabotaged my career by giving in to family pressures. What had saved me was my brother-in-law, Joey, who was always my champion while everyone else tried to convince me that secretarial school was good enough. I told Neal how Joey encouraged me and even arranged an interview for my first job.

Neal listened, took a sip of his drink and responded. But instead of sharing *his* moment, he told a banal tale of a ski trip he took ten years before with a college friend. I learned how the slopes at the resort were great but that the cuisine was lousy.

I didn't know how this had anything to do with what I'd just told him. For a second, I felt embarrassed and disappointed. What was he telling me? Was he moved by my story, but couldn't show it? Had I opened up too much with this man?

Barbara was right in feeling confused. Neal's skiing story had nothing to do with her confessional, *how I got to be where I am and who helped me.* Barbara added that she asked him, "Did something happen on that trip that had to do with your work?" He told her, "Not really . . . my friend is in advertising." Aha! An oblique connection to her business, one she had to pry out of him, but still beside the point.

At that moment, early in the relationship, Neal pretended to reveal himself to Barbara, although his anecdote was quite impersonal. In fact, he did reveal himself—to be a man who's afraid of intimacy—and Barbara should have taken notice. He didn't acknowledge her feelings about her brother-in-law, establishing a pattern that would continue throughout their relationship. Her poignant story made him feel something, which others might have shared, but not Neal. His solution was to divert her, change the subject and stop the growing intimacy dead in its tracks. Barbara ignored this warning signal, and responded to his non sequitur with a direct personal question (storming the barricades). But this too resulted in another unsatisfactory answer that left her feeling further rejected.

If you're interested in a man like Neal, you might also have tried the "confessional exchange" approach. But rather than defusing his evasiveness, you buy into it. You ignore his rejection, let the incident roll and tell yourself, as Barbara had, that Neal was "shy," or "slow to show his feelings, like many men," thereby excusing his behavior.

In all, you may blame yourself for pushing this guy into opening up. Your guilt appeals to him. It helps him feel safe. Coaxed by how you accept him and how neatly you have taken the blame, a passive-aggressive man learns he needn't make himself vulnerable to you . . . yet or ever. He's armed with the power of unlimited digressions to get you off the track. Prepare to be derailed unless you decide to make changes.

Sooner or later in relationships with passive-aggressive men, you get fed up and stop excusing their behavior. Those early signs that you chose to ignore are now staring you in the face. You can't ignore them anymore, and you want change. And you're entitled to it. Just because you once accepted certain of his passive-aggressive games doesn't mean that you have to accept them forever.

But the passive-aggressive man doesn't respond well when he feels the winds of change blowing in his direction, especially if you've taken a deep breath and want your say. Whether he is a boyfriend like Neal, a father or a boss, change frightens him and confuses him. He doesn't understand why you're protesting, why you're no longer satisfied with him. You want answers; you want him to stop his manipulations and speak to you directly; you don't like his deliberate games about being late or changing plans; you want him to be attentive rather than keep you off guard; and when he is withdrawn or angry, you don't want to let him sulk—you demand to know what's bothering him.

"He's heard it all before," a patient told me, "and so he tries to tune me out, but when he knows I mean it, that I'll leave if he doesn't change, he acts as if I'm pulling the rug out from under him."

But change can be threatening to you as well, and that explains why some women permit passive-aggression. The familiarity of the relationship may in itself be reassuring. A known quantity is comforting, which is why you may be attracted to someone like your father or brother or uncle. But it can also be a trap. Rhoda, a patient of mine, told me:

My brother was always sabotaging himself. Charlie dropped out of Harvard Law School two months before he was to graduate. He decided then he hated law. But he never found anything else. His career is the shape of a roller coaster, built by an underachiever like him—all valleys, no peaks.

On the surface, my husband seems different—Bob is more outgoing, laid-back and has great style, while Charlie's more high-strung. But they're both their own worst enemy when it comes to work. Like Charlie, Bob's professional life is a series of challenges not met, opportunities avoided. I listen to both of them complain all the time and find myself giving advice neither one takes.

Rhoda is in a place some women have shoveled themselves into: the capable woman surrounded by inept passive-aggressive men buried in their own troubles. She feels responsible for them and while she complains, she feels she's needed. Yet both men run over her. Charlie always borrows money from her and gets her involved in family-based deals that aren't thought through. Her husband is withholding and emotionally punishing whenever Rhoda proves she's better at making a living—which is every payday.

Rhoda acknowledged that changes were necessary, but she was reluctant to make demands. In therapy she realized just how threatened she was by the thought of making some changes. Not only could she not demand change from her husband or brother, but she even tried to put up barriers to prevent changes they tried to make on their own. For example, Bob finally decided to give up his high-flying hopes of starting his own business, and was offered a position at a large corporation with job security and a steady income. Rhoda advised him to reject the offer, saying she earned enough money for both of them.

Like Rhoda, many women who acknowledge that they permit passive-aggressive behavior tend to deny that they go one step further and encourage it. After all, it seems inconceivable that anyone would encourage behavior that has such a negative effect on her life. But I urge you to examine your relationships with passive-aggressive men, and see if you may be unwittingly reinforcing the passive-aggression.

Permitting—and encouraging—passive-aggression will occur unless you take the necessary self-protective measures to contain it. This means not letting yourself be taken advantage of, and most of all, setting limits and never backing down, no matter how the passive-aggressive man protests. This isn't easy. Constant vigilance is required to contain passive-aggression. You cannot let down your guard.

HOW TO PROTECT YOURSELF

People differ in regard to their tolerance for passive-aggression and their willingness to enforce limits. Certain women won't tolerate the slightest amount of passive-aggression and, when their radar detects the early-warning signs, they choose to avoid the man who exhibits them. Or, if they start a relationship with a man who turns out to be passive-aggressive, they smartly set up terms to contain his passive-aggression and limit the effect he has on them. Here's how.

LIMIT SETTING

Establishing boundaries may sound tough to do with a man who thinks the world is an extension of his fingertips, but it is actually very simple to figure out. First, be clear about what you want: what he can and can't do with you, explaining that you want him to stick to his word, be more open and follow through on his responsibilities. Next, be prepared to doggedly *hold to* the limits you set. This steadfastness is important, since it can begin to make changes in the relationship. While the goal with a passive-aggressive man is to help him to feel more empowered, this should never be at the expense of trampling over you and your interests. Victimizing you in no way empowers him, and may actually make his passive-aggression worse.

Limit setting is the policeman's role—to safeguard you from the destructive impact of his behavior. Its aim is not to rehabilitate the perpetrator. Still, it can be very effective.

At the outset, communicate to him that he cannot get away with treating you cavalierly or with disrespect. ("When you tell me a story like this, it insults me. I can hear the truth and you can tell it. It's better for both of us. . . .") Setting limits gives him an important message: that you are entitled to better treatment. Thus, setting a limit and enforcing it follows naturally. Soon a passive-aggressive man sees that he can't take advantage of you, and that you're not to be fooled.

In setting limits, always be *specific* about what bothers you, specific about your expectations, clear about your intent and willing to help him look at the consequences of his actions. To paraphrase a biblical aphorism, Hate the sin, not the sinner. Try not to tell the man he's a monster to the bone, but that his behavior is sometimes "monstrous." Or unnerving. Or counterproductive.

The tone you take is important: you want him to trust you and not feel that you are setting these limits to be vindictive, or authoritarian, as if he were the child and you the parent. One of the problems with Rhoda whose story was mentioned earlier—and who's struggling with a passive-aggressive brother and husband—is that she's overcome and exasperated by their misfired attempts and reacts shrilly. ("Can't you get things right for a change? Why do I have to bear all the burdens?")

Remember: the passive-aggressive man is driven by fear, so while he may want to walk all over you to feel stronger, paradoxically, he's also afraid that he might cause you real pain. His aggressive side may infuriate you, but underneath that is a layer of fear that is easy to sympathize with. Feeling sympathetic helps to set the right tone.

You can totally miss by using ultimatums you can't enforce. Let's take a situation, for example, where your boyfriend borrowed two hundred dollars six months ago, and has since found endless excuses to not return the money to you. Don't threaten to cancel out on a party you really want to attend. You may be punishing yourself more than him, and you're not really focusing on the problem at hand in a mature way. It only tends to escalate the conflict. Here are four other possible approaches, each one stressing a different point. You can say:

1. "I want this relationship to work, but it can only work if I can trust you with money." (A general statement about trust within the relationship), **OR**

2. "It's humiliating for me to ask you every week for what you owe me. You show no respect for me." (A statement describing how you feel), **OR**
3. "You give me one excuse after another for not paying me back, but they're just phony excuses. I want the money now." (A statement of direct confrontation), **OR**
4. "It's as if not paying me back is a way to keep me tied to you, but it does just the opposite. It makes me angry and unable to trust you. The lesson I learn is to not lend you money ever again." (A statement explaining an important consequence of his behavior)

Limit setting sounds easy in theory, but in practice, he's going to put up a real fight. He's likely to ignore what you say, or he may go along with your requests for a short time, then revert to his old self. Don't expect him to change just because you want him to, or because you summoned the strength to set limits. Keep in mind that a passive-aggressive man will try to thwart you. As in any relationship, a person with power is not about to relinquish it.

To make a change, you'll have to enforce the limits you set. If you set a limit and then behave as usual, he'll get the message that he can treat you as he likes, no matter how you balk. The passive-aggressive man has an unerring instinct for tapping the weak spot in your willpower, will exploit any hesitation on your part and will constantly challenge your resolve.

As you go through this book, you'll pick up examples of approach and limit setting for all aspects of your relationship with passive-aggressive men. And, if it should come to it, and you realize that your relationship has a poor chance of surviving, your only option may be . . .

GETTING OUT

While it might be a mistake to give up on a relationship with a passive-aggressive man until all avenues for change have been explored, at some point, you must cut your losses. If you've tried your best to contain his passive-aggression and have been unsuccessful, then you should think about getting out of the relationship or distancing yourself from him— whether he's a spouse, employer, employee, family member or friend. At some point, you may decide to break up, divorce or quit. To stay in a relationship that is harmful to you is not only pointless but self-destructive. This is one of the unfortunate costs of passive-aggression: conflicts all too quickly escalate to the point where *getting out is your only choice.*

Erica's story tells you why leaving may be the only solution. She was living with a lawyer who traveled at least one week a month. Erica could accept Jack's travel schedule, but he frequently had a packed suitcase ready at the door, making her feel that he was prepared to bolt. Jack still referred to his apartment where they both lived as *his* house, not theirs, adding to Erica's insecurity. She said to me about him:

> After three years of living together it became clear to me that Jack wasn't going to either make a commitment or acknowledge that it wasn't going to work for us—"everything suited him fine." My relationship with him was like climbing a greased pole. I always slipped and shot back to the bottom.
>
> I threatened to end the relationship, for about the tenth time, but Jack is so good at getting me to stay. He'll do anything: cajole, beg, cry and seduce his way back. This time I meant it.

Jack ignored the depth of Erica's dissatisfaction and the sincerity of her ultimatum. He took advantage of Erica's reluctance to end the relationship and bound her to him by her own dependency, blackmailing her with her own guilt.

Finally, too unhappy with Jack to go on and admitting to herself that the relationship would never improve, Erica took a step that was greater than she'd expected. She received a major promotion at work and was asked to spend a year running the company's new Chicago office. The job offer would give her the perfect out. Even though she wasn't enthusiastic about leaving New York, Erica accepted the job, with the matter of how Jack would feel still an open question.

He didn't ask her to stay. She left for Chicago, never inviting Jack to come out with her. A few months later, she called him and made it final—it was over between them.

Erica's dilemma is one of loving an intractable passive-aggressive man, one who wouldn't compromise for her. Erica's choice was simple—leave him or stay for more of the same. Since positive communication was futile, she reluctantly made the best decision *for her*.

Interestingly, Erica was able to reconcile the end of the relationship only when she was physically distanced from Jack. When I asked her why she ended it by phone, Erica replied that it would have been impossible to stick to her guns in person. If she had seen him, she said, "he would have wormed his way back into my heart . . . he's irresistible, and it kills me."

Many passive-aggressive men have a seductive quality that makes you disregard your better judgment. They play on your optimism, and romanticism—your dreams of cloudless skies and blissful love, just you and him, warm and happy. He knows what you want and he knows he can't give it to you, so he sells you promises, until the next time. And while fathers or brothers or sons or bosses don't seduce you in the same way a lover does, they still count on you to fall for how you need them or for their lovableness or how they love *you*.

Men like Jack attract a certain type of woman I call the "Rescuer" (more about women's personalities and styles in the next chapter), and Erica has a bit of this in her. She's a woman who'll make heroic efforts to salvage relationships that are doomed to failure or to rescue guys who stumble along. It doesn't work.

Once you become so enmeshed with a passive-aggressive man that you lose track of whose problem it is, breaking free is no easy business. You become closely bound together, and it is next to impossible to pull away. The key is to size up the relationship for what it gives you, not what its potential is. Too often, I see people held hostage by the hope that the passive-aggressive man will change, unwilling to acknowledge the full extent of their disappointment. Make your decision, as did Erica, based on reality, not false hope.

When Erica broke up with Jack by phone, it was the only way she could think of herself as a separate person—by literally differentiating her priorities from his and relocating. In concrete terms, she reestablished what had become blurred boundaries. Her fear of continuing as she was in an ungiving relationship helped her to take this step and keep him out of her new life in a new city. She had tried to set limits and enforce them but realized that getting out was her only answer.

A colleague once made the following glib but heartfelt remark: "The secret to dealing with a passive-aggressive man is to put him behind you. Marry him in your early twenties, and divorce him by thirty. You should learn from your mistakes, not live with them forever." Erica did.

Terminating a relationship is a wrenchingly difficult affair, especially with a relative (unless he's brutalizing and overbearing). What's most important to remember is you have a better chance of changing a relationship when you change *how you respond*—and setting limits and enforcing them tells a passive-aggressive father/brother/son that you're swimming in clearer water now and won't bite when he throws the bait. The more you are invulnerable to passive-aggressive games, the more he'll fight you. But if you stick to your guns and show self-respect, he's bound to come around. Don't expect a magical transformation, but do expect a noticeable change.

FINALLY

There is no way to be involved with anyone—a passive-aggressive man or any other person—and never want anything from him. But to be involved with a passive-aggressive man is to put yourself on an emotional seesaw from self-doubt and confusion to anger and frustration. As your expectations of him emerge bit by bit, you're bound to get into one battle or another. To avoid the battle is to lower your expectations, but then you'll hate yourself for settling for so little. Your Achilles' heel is wanting something, anything.

Another battle rages in you alone as you tough out *why he has you hooked*. What "weak spot" has he discovered in you? How did he find it? Why do you keep reacting as he wants, no matter how sore that spot gets? The next chapter continues to examine you—and why you fall for the passive-aggressive man.

3

WHO FALLS FOR THE PASSIVE-AGGRESSIVE MAN?

IF YOU'VE EVER asked yourself, "Is it my fault? Did I say or do something to provoke that response?" *the answer may be yes*. Every relationship has two players, and your role is as important as that of the passive-aggressive man. Without you, he's a man with personality problems. With you, he gets to flex his emotional muscle, feel his power, and, often, get the effect he wants.

In the previous chapter, I looked at how you may be enabling passive-aggression, consciously or unconsciously. Now I want to focus on how you present yourself—not just your style, or the degree to which you are assertive or submissive, but the subtle personality clues you drop for a passive-aggressive man to interpret.

You come to the relationship with certain inclinations, needs and emotional baggage. If the relationship isn't working (and this is why you are reading this book), *then something must give*. Good sense says to start with you, since changing yourself is within your control and easier than trying to change others. Real self-awareness helps you pinpoint why you attract and/or pursue passive-aggressive types and why you seem to permit behavior that's unsatisfying or depriving.

Your first insight will, most likely, have something to do with your own fear of separation and abandonment.

A passive-aggressive man is good at creating an illusion of *steadfastness*, a quality that's especially appealing to many women. This guy may be emotionally elusive, but he'll have you believing he's the salt of the earth, the pillar of security in your life ("I'll be home tonight. Call me if you need *anything*. If I'm out, it's just for half an hour, so try again. . . ."). Whatever else his faults may be and no matter how difficult he is to deal with, a passive-aggressive man is *there*. It's his most admirable, and most diabolical, quality. His rootedness is both reassuring, and a curse, to women who get involved with him.

What's likely to happen is that you make a tacit deal with him, negotiating a trade-off between security and fulfillment. He's the personality type least likely to reject you directly. However, his passive-aggression may be the excessive price you pay until you're able to change.

Let's now look at why you may have wittingly or unwittingly fallen for passive-aggressive men. The behavioral "types" that follow—Victim, Rescuer and Manager—describe a particular personality inclination that seems to attract passive-aggressive men.

THE VICTIM

The passive-aggressive man has true power over the woman who lets herself be run by him. Operating from a poor sense of self-worth and a fragmented self-image, the Victim, sadly, is an abuse collector to her passive-aggressive man's role of abuse giver. Whether she believes that a whole man with half a heart is good enough for her or better than nothing, the Victim enters a relationship with a passive-aggressive man with little chance that the relationship will improve. He is happy to reinforce the doubts she has about her value as a person, her sexuality, her sociability or her mind.

Victims may be sensitive women, but often, they're hesitant

about communicating their feelings. Ironically, they're as afraid of completely revealing themselves as are the men from whom they seek comfort, backup support or love. When they can talk about what bothers them, Victims are likely to apologize for *having* feelings ("I'm sorry I took your time to tell you this ridiculous story. . . .").

Underneath it all, they are seething and frightened, fearing loneliness and being without love, but at the same time they cherish the distance passive-aggressive men create so nicely for them. Life may be unpleasant at times, but it's safe, in its unsettling way. Since the passive-aggressive man's agenda is to keep a woman off balance, the Victim is a perfect foil—she tips over at the slightest touch.

Many Victims don't understand why they've been pushed. They feel they're the giving ones and that others prey on their generosity and kind heart. This is true in many cases: they do give, but they also set themselves up *to lose*. They know they are giving to people who will never reciprocate, care or communicate in any meaningful way. ("How did this happen again? Taking a job with a killer who overworks and under-pays me!")

Connecting with a passive-aggressive man has its benefits for the Victim: he's a familiar player, probably one in a life-time of passive-aggressive figures. Take Jane's case. At twenty-nine, she had been engaged twice, but returned the rings to each man a few months before the wedding. When I met her, she was deep into the third important relationship in her life, a conscious attempt, she told me, at breaking her predilection for "workaholics" who "squeeze me into their busy sched-ules." With George, she hoped to give herself a chance with "a nice guy."

During our therapy sessions, I saw how the men in Jane's life were essentially interchangeable: they were all self-in-volved and passive-aggressive, including her nice guy, George. A former folk-singer who had never quite made it, George got a degree and was teaching college math. From Jane's reports about him, George seemed to be as indirect, out of touch with his feelings, manipulative and withholding as the "establishment types" he had contempt for and ridiculed in song. Jane was still the doormat, but George composed no songs about that.

I asked Jane what most characterized these three men, all of whom she had considered marrying. She said:

> They had a way of making me feel that I was not good enough for them. When they said they loved me, I was unconvinced. . . . I always thought I was being fooled. But I thought if I could win their love . . . that would make me special. It didn't work. I never felt that any of them truly loved me.

In the many incidents she described to me, each man was revealed as having a low threshold for intimacy and a high threshold for frustrating Jane. The hardest on Jane was their "emotional backlash"—whenever they allowed themselves to be vulnerable or giving, they'd mete out a kind of emotional torment over the subsequent few weeks for having been loving. What they gave, they canceled out.

Since they were panicked by displays of deep emotion, openly abusing Jane made them feel strong and less dependent on her. This made Jane believe that they did not need her or love her and were thinking of leaving her.

Each man was a classic passive-aggressive. When I pointed this out, Jane didn't seem surprised that she'd fallen into a pattern, and one with a name. In fact, in her mind, she made a further connection: the traits she so disliked in the men she'd loved oddly reflected the traits she'd grown up with; the traits formed a composite profile of her mother.

Jane's mother, typical of her generation, was a bright woman who subverted her ambition and curiosity in the world to fit into a conventional mold and "make a home" for her husband. The need for acceptability and the fear of what others thought of her and her family ran the woman's life. Jane's father had a successful suburban contracting business and left most of his daughters' rearing to his wife. Jane was his favored child—it was a fact she knew from earliest childhood, but it was rarely openly expressed between them.

In the course of therapy, Jane came to admit openly—and confront—an important piece of information: she subconsciously associated love with humiliation, empty promises and the power of what is not said aloud. To Jane, love was love when it appeared as a suggestion or a reward for accepting other people's ungivingness; love was love when it was *less*, not more. And she'd learned this about love from her first source, her mother, a paradigm of the withholding, passive-aggressive personality, and her father, who while being a more giving man, did not know how to express affection without being embarrassed by it.

What helped Jane most was seeing how the patterns in her relationships with men evolved out of her early life. Growing up with a mother who was easily threatened and full of criticism, Jane didn't learn how to make her needs known and gratified. Since deprivation was on her mother's menu day after day, Jane grew up believing that she could expect a lifetime of empty plates from others, too. If you think that others will give you love only when they so choose, not when you need it or ask for it—as happened in Jane's growing up— as you wait, so do you suffer. If you believe, as Jane did, that fate will punish you by taking the one you love from you, then you never experience the pleasure of love while you have it.

Jane always put herself in the Victim's role with men: the man's needs were first, hers were last and the gap between the two was wide. To narrow that gap, Jane changed giving into *giving in*. She set up no-win situations for herself because she didn't speak up when someone offended her. She couldn't say, for example, "Don't cancel out on me ten minutes before we're supposed to go out," "Why start a fight again before we go to bed?" or "If you're short of cash, why accuse me of making excessive financial demands on you?" If she brought the matter up at all, and most times she didn't, it would be after the fact, and predictably, the man involved would make light of her complaint.

Victims let themselves be pushed around. When they set

limits, they are loath to enforce them. Passive-aggressive guys learn to ignore ultimatums, especially those laid down by the powerless Victim. They continue acting as if they care, knowing, as in Jane's case, that she would never leave. But Jane was not wholly a Victim, and managed to rescue herself before she married each of these men. Unfortunately, she hadn't had sufficient insight to stop the pattern earlier.

The answer to Jane's problem lies with Jane herself and what she can do to reclaim self-esteem and regain her dignity. Jane has finally begun to learn that *abuse is not love*, but that love can be abused and used as a weapon against her. She can now distinguish loving attention and care from grudging attention and despair. As she feels entitled to real love, Jane won't settle for less and allow herself to be mistreated. It's up to her to realize that happiness with a man is not tantamount to bondage—that loving a man does not mean she'll become too dependent on him.

If you're stuck in the same place as Jane, you can finally break loose from the Victim's role. Understand that you haven't been singled out for punishment or deprivation or a lifetime of struggling for pennies at a company that doesn't appreciate you.

In a fascinating article on Jean Harris, the socialite girls' school headmistress who shot Scarsdale doctor Herman Tarnower, reporter Ellen Goodman speculated on why Harris killed him after a tempestuous fourteen-year relationship: "Harris had learned too well how to swallow mouthfuls of humiliation in return for tidbits of attention. . . . She is Everywoman who ever hung onto a relationship by her fingernails while her self-esteem eroded like a crumbly windowsill on the eighteenth floor."

Jean Harris lived the Victim role with a womanizing, noncommittal Lothario she hoped her helpless love would change. It didn't work. If all you get is the crumbs or if you see your relationship crumbling away, save your own life. Believe your life is ashes, and you remain the Victim. Give it up and you know the freedom of building a life of your own making.

Every relationship is different, but what the best ones have in common is *choice*—choosing to be together, daily *inviting each other into each other's life*. Jane still has far to go in strengthening her self-esteem, but with her newfound awareness of the kind of men to avoid, I have faith in her future.

THE MANAGER

Women involved with passive-aggressive men tell me they wish their partners would feel comfortable enough with them to speak their minds openly and honestly. Sounds reasonable, since openness implies total freedom to agree or disagree with each other. "Let him assert himself more," they say. "How about less dodging the issue, less of a need to diminish everyone's feelings, including his own? How about more decisiveness?"

These terms sound fair and even magnanimous, but, I've discovered along the way, the interest some women actually have in open communication is *not* always genuine. Unspoken fears and reservations get in their way, too, and they're often as timid about intimacy as the men they want it from. They're women I call Managers, *who cannot take no for an answer*. Since the suggestion of openness to them is as threatening as an approaching fist, the Manager squelches intimacy and turns to *control*.

What happens? A passive-aggressive man may at first be willing to assert himself or tell you how he feels, but communication stops, ironically, with *you*. Possibly afraid of what you might hear, you interrupt him, subtly letting him know that you disapprove. Later, he won't go on, and you can't pry the words out of him. In another scenario, the passive-aggressive man goes so far as to tell you *no*, he won't do what you want, but you can't or won't accept his answer, and keep pushing for a "yes." The conversation trails off, and he becomes sullen; he may even capitulate, but resent it for long afterward.

For the Manager, getting her way is much more important

than hearing what the man has to say. Audrey is a good case in point.

Frank and Audrey are typical of a couple who lead parallel lives in too many ways, intersecting only at highly charged emotional crossroads. Frank is my patient, a true passive-aggressive man, but I've met and spoken to his wife, Audrey, the model of a classic Manager who's created her own passive-aggressive Frankenstein. Audrey is controlling and embittered; Frank timid and obstinate. She points to Frank as the source of her miseries, while he quietly feels sorry for himself.

Audrey, it's my guess, holds a silent grudge against Frank. While he's more easygoing than she and not as slickly self-confident as many fast-track types, Frank's mild manner serves him well. He's a successful enough accountant on an upward career path and a likable guy. Audrey is harder on people and more demanding, her manner belying a basic insecurity. The chink in Audrey's armor is her fear of separation. A part of her totally relies on Frank, but he's not generous about it. Instead, he plays on it, taking advantage of her fears, quietly daring her to walk out. Audrey, however, thinks she'd fail on her own, especially with two children under ten years old to care for. This only fuels her attempts to control Frank, as she places greater and greater demands on him.

One of Audrey's complaints about Frank is that, at times, she believes she is entitled to a straightforward answer, or a conversation that would allay many of her fears and insecurities. But Frank provides neither. He sidesteps the issue, withholding reassurance. What Audrey doesn't recognize is that there are also times when she refuses to listen to what Frank has to say. So are there times when Frank might offer his response—a timid "No, not right now" or "No, I don't want to"—clear signals that should tell Audrey to pay attention.

The part of Audrey that needs to ignore Frank's *no* needs to humiliate him, too. What gets her is that Frank takes her insults like a wimp, with no apparent retaliation. Audrey doesn't make the connection that Frank's passive-aggression—playing on her insecurities, avoiding intimacy—is his response. His anger comes out at a later date and in an indirect way but still has unfortunate consequences for her.

Their marital problems didn't start with Audrey's envy of Frank's abilities to negotiate the workplace, but in the early stages of establishing their relationship. A pattern was set up back then: she would ask him for something, he would refuse it and she would keep at him, throwing in a few insults to boot. Eventually, Frank *wouldn't answer her at all*. Since Audrey wouldn't accept no for an answer, he would find other ways to avoid her demands, whether it by silence, walking out of the room or changing the subject. Passive-aggression in action.

When Audrey had leverage over Frank, she would succeed in extracting his compliance, getting her way without concern for what Frank thought. She loved him but resented him; she provoked his hostility but wouldn't confront it, or hers. More like a Manager than a wife, Audrey desexualized Frank, banishing him from their bed to the living-room sofa more often than not because his "snoring kept her awake." Frank would passively submit to the exile. At first, he was hurt and humiliated, but over time it suited him to keep his distance. Then *he* became the one in control: when she wanted sex, he wasn't available. He moved to the sofa permanently and communication between them deteriorated further.

Caught up in her dissatisfaction in work and love, Audrey perpetuated her frustration and rage by demeaning Frank. Audrey declared that she wanted Frank to be more forceful, to tell her when he was dissatisfied, but other truths were in operation. As much as she complained about him, it was she who exacerbated his problem by making him feel that it was *unacceptable* for him to want the things he wanted. And what he wanted was his needs taken care of and to be accepted. He became reluctant to articulate in what way, and Audrey felt put upon by a man who was too vague and circuitous to be honest with his own wife. He felt neglected and misunderstood. The vicious circle closed.

The real dialogues between Audrey and Frank are the conversations that are *never* held—the unspoken subtexts, suggestions, misread signals, misunderstood comments and the ignored, and often broad, hints. When a man who's not good at speaking his mind and who has a tendency to obstruct things for the hell of it is confronted by a Manager who wants to control him, the relationship has no other course but to grind to a standstill.

In this case, Audrey may have appeared to be ahead: basically, she got what she wanted from Frank, a passively compliant guy. But there were so many things missing that life was never fully satisfying for her. Playing "tough guy" to his "patsy" was a dead end—all his passive-aggression allowed her was to put off dealing with her helpless sense of dependency on him and kept her stuck where she was.

If you've found yourself becoming a Manager, like Audrey you'll get more from *any* relationship with a passive-aggressive man—in love, at work or in your family—if you're willing to make some changes within yourself. The only way to have a truly honest interaction is when you're willing to acknowledge a few truths.

First, if you're like Audrey, you need to look at how you slip into controlling others, probably because you're threatened by his autonomy. *The person who is free to say no is also free to go.* Let's take Audrey's case again. Since she fears such independence in a man, she stifles or ignores it. She fears Frank will leave her, so she undermines and weakens him, and, up to now, he's taken it. By playing the Manager and not taking *no* for an answer, Audrey creates for herself the role of domineering "mother," fulfilling the passive-aggressive man's worst fantasies of being entrapped by a devouring, all-powerful woman.

Secondly, Managers must be prepared to take *no* for an answer. Sometimes, it's not easy to hear "no," and with good reason. I understand how you feel rejected; you want your own way, but the other person won't agree, even if yours is clearly the best answer. But such "no's" don't go away. Until you're willing to accept his "no," however unjustifiable or disappointing it may be, you'll set up situations for the passive-aggressive man to express it in less direct and far more devious and irritating ways.

Each one of us is entitled to say no: *no!* we do not want to visit the in-laws yet again this Sunday afternoon; *no!* we do not want to get married or get married *again; no!* we don't want to pick up the check again for dinner; *no!* we don't want to get stuck doing all the work because everyone else has "more important things to do"; and *no!* you cannot cut my hair as you like because you're holding the scissors!

The passive-aggressive man has a problem saying *no* to you, but it just may be because you need to hear "yes." What you end up with is more passive-aggression.

THE RESCUER

As there is a specific problem within a relationship for the Manager, so is there a similar kind of tension for the Rescuer. Both women deal with passive-aggressive men from the position of *custodian*. The Manager, being a "woman who can't take no for an answer" wants the upper hand; she often openly conducts herself as a person in control, maneuvering the passive-aggressive man into her thrall.

The Rescuer is usually far less strident in her style, but equally as directorial. She can appear in the guise of Earth Mother, keeper of the flame, the "woman behind the man," the fixer, the support system, the siren, the giver of all that is warm and good.

The Rescuer sees the passive-aggressive man on the brink of disaster—in his career or in his personal life—and her natural impulse is to help someone who's down. She comes in to save the day. The passive-aggressive man is beguiled . . . and submits. He may even have invited it. At first, he loves the attention.

The Rescuer's motives may, on the surface, appear well-intentioned and often they are; but just as often, they aren't all so virtuous and altruistic. For a passive-aggressive man, such generosity is not liberating but enslaving. As a Rescuer, your job is to make him look good to the outside world—you are a soldier ready to do battle for his ego. You make excuses for his laziness, his lateness, his clumsiness as you take over what you can, reminding him, "That's okay, Herb. I can get it done faster anyway." As he screws up, so do you clean up after him. As he backs down, spoiled by your attentiveness or *knowing you will make things right*, you take over and keep him going.

Such overprotection takes an emotionally serpentine path through this relationship, whether it's business or personal. If you find more maternity than equality, perspicacity and sexuality in your relationship than you care to measure, you need to figure out what you're getting out of the Rescuer's role. If the guy is self-destructive—he has a hard time keeping a job or getting promoted; he's got an alcohol or drug problem; he is socially inept or so challenging that you're his only friend—how far do you go in the role of helpmate?

If he's basically middle-of-the-road, not extreme in any of the above problems, but maddening in his carelessness—he loses keys, important papers; he goes to make a phone call at the airport and forgets to take his suitcase on the plane; he smokes and has burned holes in every piece of upholstered furniture and all the lapels of his jackets; he never finishes any task he starts or lives in dreams he wants you to actualize for him—how much do you attend to him and his possessions like a mother hen?

Mark and Rita had to deal with a conflict like this—the Rescuer and her competence versus the Rescued, her Mr. Magoo–like boyfriend who was oblivious to the dangers that surrounded him. Generally low-key and rarely ruffled, Mark was a fairly secure stockbroker of thirty-four with a few passive-aggressive traits, most notably, habitual procrastination, absentmindedness, and a naïveté that people found annoying and that moved Rita to hover over him.

Rita, a more vital and extroverted person, was, at thirty years old, more attentive to the details of living and manners.

She worried that Mark would be so involved in reading the paper he'd forget to get off at the right subway stop; she feared that he'd be mugged, say something sarcastic to the mugger and be killed on the street; she worried about how to get him to give up the idea of redoing the walk-in closet, probably inconveniencing both of them for *another* eight months; she worried because sex was becoming more infrequent and less passionate.

In many ways, Mark and Rita meshed well, but lately, Rita was complaining about Mark's passive-aggression. At a session in my office, she revealed how she'd become a Rescuer to Mark. Rita, who tended to be outspoken and often histrionically dramatized events, felt that Mark often set her up to look like the "bad guy" among their friends. This infuriated her since she was "always trying to make him happy," or "trying to get the best out of him."

By concentrating on Mark's "inadequacies," Rita tended to ignore or downplay her contribution to their cooling relationship. She hovered over Mark as if he were a mildly handicapped child and she was his arms, legs and directional signals. In effect, Rita behaved as if she were his *mother*—infantilizing and desexualizing him at the same time.

A man made to feel incompetent is not far from impotent—and angry about it. By turning him into a child, she overplayed her protective instinct and lost him as a man. She told me:

> I've lost respect for Mark. How can anyone respect a man they have to baby all the time?
>
> So many questions come to me: Why did I choose such a man to begin with . . . a guy who could forget his own name, a guy who could really annoy me with his twists of reality, a guy who could turn off emotionally at the drop of a hat. Why on earth did I want to stay with him?

As I talked with Rita, a number of the reasons became clear. She depended on Mark's reliability—he was always there, the steady presence—and however much she complained, she wanted him to stay that way. He could organize her and calm her down. There were none of the incendiary arguments she used to have in prior relationships with men who were as outspoken as she. In fact, Rita discouraged Mark from expressing his hostility more directly.

Rita had worries other than whether or not Mark would find his way home. When they entered therapy with me, she worried that Mark did not love her. Not yet able to accept the distinction between building confidence in others and allowing their independence and rescuing and controlling them, Rita held on to her Rescuer's approach to Mark. In fact, Rita wasn't ready for Mark to change and be less passive-aggressive.

When you act like the parent or authority figure to a passive-aggressive man, when you assume his responsibilities or make decisions for him, then you have encouraged him to play a dependent role. At some very basic level, you've enabled him to be passive-aggressive.

If you are the kind of wife/mother/sister who fixes the sink herself or calls a plumber rather than remind the guy of the job he'd promised to do—*you are just such an enabler.* By not wanting to stir the waters of adversity, you reinforce a passive-aggressive man's contrariness, and make it unlikely that he'll fix the plumbing in the future—or fix it within any reasonable time. You'll always be left with the dirty work. And the passive-aggressive man will have all the more reason to perceive you as "domineering" and resent the power you have.

An unhealthy symbiosis can grow out of the Rescuer/Rescued relationship, and you wind up colluding (if unconsciously) with the passive-aggressive man in trying to keep the conflicts going. Ironically, his passive-aggressiveness protects *you* from the anxiety of changing.

It's difficult to watch someone either destroy his life (the extreme cases) or stumble through blunder after blunder, and not do something to help. Such failures probably have re-percussions that directly affect you. To rescue or not to res-cue—neither option is really right. Beyond the personal pain, a passive-aggressive man will see your unwillingness to rescue him as a rejection, reinforcing the perception of you as not caring enough about him. On the other hand, the more you mother him, and the more he allows it, the more both of you have accepted his basic incompetence and inadequacy.

It's only by giving him breathing space to make his own mistakes that he'll learn to grow up.

The passive-aggressive man is difficult, he's vulnerable and, as you've learned, a bit clumsy around women. But if you want his commitment, cooperation and/or affection and feel you're fighting him for it, you need a different approach to him.

By recognizing in yourself the qualities of the Victim or the Manager or the Rescuer, you can see why you fell for a passive-aggressive man. But his expectations of you will change as you alter how you act with him. So if you have a history of permitting passive-aggression, you've still got a good chance to stop what's hurting you and build better relationships.

4

THE PASSIVE-AGGRESSIVE
MAN: GROWING UP AND
GETTING THAT WAY

I'VE OFTEN BEEN asked to put together a complete portrait of the passive-aggressive man—a neat blueprint that maps the routes his problems take. It's not so easy a task as you might guess, since every man is different, each story is unique and a guy who copes with life by using passive-aggressive tactics isn't a simple personality. Still, as varied a character as he is, a number of recurrent patterns from his early life can help answer the question, *How did he get this way?* A number of theories exist.

LANDSCAPE AND BLOODLINE: SOCIOLOGICAL AND BIOLOGICAL CAUSES

How much of who we are is *where we're from* versus *who we're from*? It is a much-debated question that asks if environment or genetics, or what particular balance of the two—"nature versus nurture" or nature *and* nurture—is responsible for the person we are today.

The controversy creates an endless range of possibilities. There's no guarantee that, for example, brothers raised in a working-class home by highly moral parents who made the same financial sacrifices for each of them will turn out alike. In fact, as adults, they can be as different from one another as a Georgia peanut farmer is from his counterpart in the Hindu Kush.

Most psychologists, however, do hold to a two-component definition of personality. Some have a stronger bias toward "nature," some for "nurture." We take into consideration, first, *temperament*, believed to spring from genetic factors, and, second, *adaptive character*, the result of environmental and cultural influences.

"Nature" would surely begin with *genes*, the irrevocable influence that creates human life. Genes, encoded in DNA, describe the "predetermined" aspect of humanity. Although they are responsible for how you respond, even *they* are not the whole story, only a fascinating chapter in the evolution of personality. Some passive-aggressive men think the key to their personality *is* genetics, and that it will be science's mission to find the "master switch" to turn it off or on again. One patient married to a passive-aggressive man told me:

> Carl has a theory about people, based on their noses. He believes the men with the shorter flatter noses *like his* are colder, tougher, and better businessmen. Others, like his father, have hook noses and are more easygoing, but have a harder time making it.
> He takes this nose-disposition correlation as gospel, and believes that his personality is unchangeable. So why bother with therapy, he says!

Personal (and scientific) observation confirms the theory that there exist distinct and innate differences in disposition even in newborn babies. These temperamental inclinations and nuances persist from infancy throughout life. A basically tranquil nature, a crankiness, coolness or low frustration level—and even tendencies to antisocial behavior—have been traced to heredity. The breeding of a sociopathic "bad seed" or a high-energy, gregarious performer or a pious "church lady"—to use just three examples—is no longer simply a dramatic concept, but one that has some basis in fact. However, it doesn't reveal the whole story, since genes alone do *not* make the person.

If there is one difficulty scientists have in pinpointing the biological roots of passive-aggression it's that it is too complex to be reduced to simple molecules, hormones or system of brain neurotransmitters.

And then there's "nurture"—socialization via the influence of schools, trends, friends, economics, television, advertising and *so much more* are responsible for shaping personality. Systems of law and social order try to fit man in with those around him, setting up cultural and civil contexts that are intended to perpetuate and protect that society. Through "nurture," man finds his place in that society. Psychologists investigate what kind of social structures create passive-aggression, whether it is greater in a country like Japan, which demands compliance and respect for authority, or in the United States, with its mavericks and rebels. There is no real answer yet. But "nurture" exerts its greatest influence through parental caretaking, which is the reason psychologists focus on child development.

"The child is the father to the man" means that one's early experiences, the contexts in which they occur and the interpretation given them provide a reasonable foundation for figuring out personality development. It's a shaky foundation for the elusive passive-aggressive man. He's stuck in his past, so emotionally fragile he uses insensitivity to others and self-deception as a shield to protect himself against the world. Let's take a look at his early history and see where those barriers might have first gone up.

BECOMING PASSIVE-AGGRESSIVE: AN OVERVIEW

Life stories are said to have been written because of a single traumatic event—early childhood abandonment by a parent, a sudden violent act, touching the hand of a hero, public humiliation, a moment of clarity when you recognize your future! It's always tempting to seek that isolated event in your life that seems to capture the essence of *why* you are who you are and behave as you do. Rarely, though, can one incident be singled out as the cause of passive-aggressive behavior.

What anyone can know about the passive-aggressive man's childhood mostly comes from his telling of his own history—we rarely get to speak in depth to his parents, siblings, teachers or pals for corroboration or another point of view. Since "the facts" come exclusively from his point of view, most psychologists tend to view his life history as fairly vulnerable to distortions.

This isn't unusual—we all perceive the world uniquely. Two men may each win one thousand dollars in a lottery; one man will rejoice and plan how to spend it, another will resent the tax bite on the added income, think only of how much less he has to sock away in the bank and feel cheated. So while situations may be identical, the *interpretations* we bring to them always differ.

In psychotherapy, the historical reality of your childhood, that is, the *accuracy* of remembered details, is generally considered secondary in importance. The focus is on how you see things, the emotional significance of your memories. It is this so-called "psychic reality" that actually influences and shapes your thinking and behavior.

I agree that it is important to differentiate between how a child *perceives* his parents' actions and how they actually behaved toward him. Because a passive-aggressive man felt needy and controlled does not mean that his parents did, in fact, withhold either affection or approval. Nor were they necessarily overbearing. It is easy to blame parents, but they aren't entirely accountable for their son's behavior and, by extension, for his becoming passive-aggressive.

What's more important is how he behaves with them, and to a lesser extent, how he deals with other caretakers and siblings—and how these behavior patterns carry into the relationships he forms throughout life. If you've ever been exasperated by a passive-aggressive man who gives you the "silent treatment," you can be sure the gambit has traveled with him from childhood.

The choice he makes as a boy to use the silent treatment might have once been a protective and adaptive response to a parent. The possible scenario: his father demands obedience and won't listen to his point of view ("Who are you to know anything or to tell me what *you* want?") or his mother capriciously humiliates him when he takes a stand for what he wants ("Some little boys think they're so smart, don't they?"). Hurt by his mother or father, he expresses—and *denies*—anger in the only way he knows how: silence. It's one of the only areas over which he can exercise control.

Silence might have seemed the only effective defense—why speak when his words already fell on deaf ears or were used as weapons against him? The choice to swallow an opinion or not show his feelings with friends/teammates/teachers as a boy can perpetuate itself over a lifetime. When he's a grown man, he'll arm himself with the "silent treatment," against lovers, spouses, friends and bosses, believing they have the power to hurt him much as his parents did. By this time, the use of silence and withdrawal are no longer adaptive but deeply ingrained.

Here is an example. You go for a job interview and face a man who creates an air of discomfort by being silent too long between questions/answers or who looks at you—or looks through you—without saying a word. As women have told me, "There are men who make me do all the talking until I'm babbling hysterically to break the ice." What they really want to say is: "You don't have to be such a cold fish with me—I'm not your mother." But rare is the person who can actually be so blunt.

There are many fixed styles of coping and relating to others that develop early on in the life of a passive-aggressive man. Many of these learned patterns and interactions originate with parent and child, occur day in and day out and, obviously, have the most profound influence on his personality.

Let's take it step by step, and see what may have happened as the passive-aggressive man grew up.

FIRST CLUES: EARLY CHILDHOOD AND PASSIVE-AGGRESSION

One major problem for a woman involved with a passive-aggressive man is his *inconsistency*. He's self-sufficient, having you believe you're nothing, but he's also scared, needs you, and claims you're his lifeboat. You must walk a fine line in figuring out how best to respond to him. What's it all about? In part, his *conflict over dependency*. (It's so serious an issue for the passive-aggressive man that I'll take a closer look at it in the next chapter.)

Where does it begin? A baby is wholly dependent on his parents for survival when he's born, and he'll be dependent on them in one way or another until he leaves their house to make his own life *independently*. Yet, long after early dependency needs are outgrown, problems may persist. They stem from an early sense of deprivation, sometimes so intensely felt that it affects everything the passive-aggressive man does.

Many passive-aggressive men remember childhood as being a time of deprivation *and* inconsistency (the same thing that dogs him now). Even when his parents couldn't do enough for him, they never cared the way he wanted them to. This still troubles him. Since he subconsciously expects to be treated by others as his parents treated him, it's not unlikely that he'll find deprivation where there is none. Nothing is enough, and disappointments prove his point. Any oversight on your part brings out accusations, such as, "You never do anything for me . . . no one does anything for me!"

He may even set up situations that *invite* others to deprive or reject him, further proving that others aren't giving. It's what we mean by a "self-fulfilling prophecy." It's how patterns are established over time and become second nature. Yet, to compensate for this feeling of being deprived, the passive-aggressive man also thinks he's *entitled* to special treatment. In a way, he feels his early wounds justify his selfishness now, with you.

Life histories of passive-aggressive men are notable for the tales of stubbornness and lack of cooperation at a very early age. Parents have clear-cut expectations of how a child should behave, and they try to get the child to comply through elaborate rewards and/or punishments. The young passive-aggressive man feels these expectations demand too much of him and that his parents are either too controlling or too quick to punish.

When you're a child, parents have all the power. The passive-aggressive man finds it an intolerable burden on him. To comply ("Be a good boy, and . . .") is proof of his weakness, and by refusing to heed his parents' wishes, many a passive-aggressive man starts his pattern of being contrary, especially to authority. Other personality traits (like stubbornness) develop and are tested for effect about this time. These traits are the forerunners of more sophisticated patterns, both conscious and unconscious, that passive-aggressive men bring with them to nearly all relationships—being withholding, overly controlling, manipulative, evasive and self-destructive.

As a child grows and gains physical strength and coordination, he develops mobility. He can freely and safely move around on his own, giving himself a sense of command in the universe. When he can walk around without assistance, the toddler feels some control over his destiny. No longer entirely dependent on his parents for support, he can make choices that test his body and the scope of his curiosity. He can leave one room and explore another space and figure out how to grasp what he reaches for. As the world opens up to him and extends beyond his fingertips, this new autonomy offers great opportunities, but it poses dangers as well.

This is the phase of child development that packs another emotional wallop: "separation/individuation." It's when a child begins to conceive of himself as distinctly himself, not an appendage to mother, but not quite yet "me." Unsure of himself, he vacillates between a genuine inclination for independence and the need for his parents' continual protection. He may roam around for short periods of time, but he'll check to make sure his mother is where he left her. This "rapprochement" has a twofold meaning: checking up on his mother acknowledges his dependency on her and clearly shows his anxiety about being separated from her. Despite his wish for freedom, he needs reassurance from a familiar and trusted figure.

Separation anxiety hits parents too: they worry about their son growing up and growing away from them, ever struggling with the question of how much freedom to give him and when/where/how to set limits and controls. If he gets too much freedom, he may not know how to handle it without putting himself in jeopardy. If he gets too little, he may never develop the skills that are crucial for him to function effectively as an adult. A passive-aggressive man falls somewhere between the two extremes of dealing with freedom, but what's on target is his still unresolved conflicts and fears associated with dependency.

When these fears resonate decades later, most men, like Dan, a patient of mine, can point to patterns developed in their childhoods that influence how they behave now. Dan is a successful account executive with a major advertising agency, committed to his job and a taskmaster of a boss, but he's unable to have a trusting relationship with women, including Arlene, the woman he lives with. Expressions of affection or intimacy, in fact, most of his feelings, tend to lie, as he describes it, "entrapped" within him.

This reminiscence from his childhood tells why: Dan's mother would *pin down* his blankets to the mattress pad to prevent him "from falling out of bed." Basically, he was pinned as tightly into his quilt cocoon as a newborn infant bound in a bunting. It was his mother's nightly habit until he was about five years old, years past the age that any normal child would require being "cribbed" in. The image came to Dan quite suddenly one afternoon, and in recalling it, he responded viscerally, becoming momentarily flushed and pan-icky.

It's a fascinating incident because while it doesn't fully answer the question of why Dan relates to women as he does, it frames the basis of a problem he's struggling with now: Dan perceives of marriage—or even intimacy with a woman—as his final *capture*. Small wonder.

The other part of the child-rearing equation is Dan's father. The man took a backseat role as an active parent, believing that small boys need their mother, growing-boys-into-men need their father. Unfortunately, by the time Dan hit twelve or thirteen, he and his father established a relationship based on distance, not intimacy. Both men were always uncomfortable in each other's presence, or angry about something vague, belying the real affection they had for each other. Neither one was very good at changing things between them, even now.

This early assault on his ego affects how Dan responds to women: situations that suggest too much intimacy make him feel as if he's in jeopardy—more to the point, "pinned down." He said:

> My mother's fingerprints were heavy on me. I know all women aren't her, but that doesn't seem to matter. I'm afraid to lose it with a woman.

Not every passive-aggressive man goes through such vividly dramatic episodes as Dan. But what these men *do* have in common is that, as boys, they're made to feel insecure about leaving their mothers, and as adults, they are ashamed of their wish for independence. As successful as Dan may be in his career, *inside* he still harbors serious doubts about his ability to go it alone in the world. His mother's voice is still resonating, reminding him of external dangers that could threaten him without her control. And then there is his father, the obedient chauffeur to his mother's backseat driving. His modus operandi was "peace at any cost."

What happens? A passive-aggressive man like Dan can break off what he thinks is a relationship that "traps" and stifles him, strike out on his own, date other women, then strike out with *them*. Overwhelmed by all his freedom, he's likely to return to the safety of his original, "entrapped" but very dependent relationship. He'll call it something else, though. He's likely to say: "I don't get 'the new woman' these days." "Why start over when all women are basically the same?" "No one is perfect, so I don't think I'm compromising by going back to Brenda." It's as if he's testing how far away he can go, only to realize that it isn't very far.

Profound conflicts often exist about his mother: as much as he may love her, he fears her and any woman who reminds him of her. And all women do. Passive-aggressive men are likely to re-create unsatisfactory relationships, if only because they have a familiarity to them, even if it is an *awful* familiarity. Often, you are an unwitting player in his reconstruction of his past.

Let's say his mother needed to know his every move. This is the emotional fact he holds on to. Now he's with you and believes you dog his trail, too. He'll twist information and events to prove himself right. How? First it's his move. He's vague about when he can see you Friday night and asks you to "hang loose." You hang loose, and he's nowhere to be found by ten o'clock. You leave messages with his service; he calls you back at eleven, annoyed that you called four times to see where he is. And so he has his proof: you are possessive.

A part of him cherishes his mother's care and attention, and he still may yearn for it, but now that he is grown up, the tables are turned: he gets to control how much power a woman has over him. He'll use all his charm, his self-dramatizing tales of woe, his suppressed fury and his empty promises to get you to work for his approval, love and acceptance. The dependency/power game he plays wobbles on a shaky emotional base, but starts to become ingrained as he grows up.

MIDDLE CHILDHOOD: GROWING UP AND FITTING IN

By the time a boy is eight or nine years old, his opportunities for negotiating the world as an individual with opinions, instinct and some knowledge about the mean streets increase enormously. Conflicts over competition, the classical Oedipal "crisis" (opposition with his father), observing his parents' relationship and making judgments about how they behave toward each other, getting along in school and sibling rivalry, take on great importance.

Let's start with his view of his parents' marriage. Typically, there is a history of strife between them, whether manifested by open warfare and door slamming or by "détente," coolness and excessive self-consciousness. "When I was about nine years old," a passive-aggressive patient told me, "I asked my mother if she believed in God. She said not to ask such personal questions."

A remarkably high rate of alcoholism exists among the parents of passive-aggressive men. Alcohol has a way of facilitating conflict. A tempestuous fight is one way to create distance. The child caught in the emotional fray is either an impotent observer of his parents' battle or a victim in the clash. The passive-aggressive man learns how to fight his "cold wars"—that wary peace he's made with *you* and intimacy—from his parents.

Wildly conflicted about his mother, especially if she was strong-willed and married to a father who was either humiliated by her or absent too often, the passive-aggressive man grew up lacking a suitable male role model. If his mother devalued his father, then to be like him was to be contemptible.

This leaves identification with his mother, who was feared and resented. Yet to take his mother's side as an ally against his father precipitates too much guilt. To win the Oedipal competition—usurping his father's position, in Freudian terms—is taboo. So the passive-aggressive man winds up vacillating between identifying with his father—a man he doesn't fully respect—and shying away from his coldness, wrath or apathy.

Some parents communicate with each other only through their son, their conversations limited to exchanges about how to handle him. Other parents speak around him, as if he were an object. One passive-aggressive man told me that his boyhood was spent being "disappeared" by his father. He might be sitting in the living room with his parents, past his normal bedtime. Rather than speak directly to him, his father would remind his mother, "Tell the boy to go to bed." Ron told me, "There was a spookiness to it . . . as if I didn't exist." As a child, the passive-aggressive man was more talked *about* in his own presence than talked *to*.

Reluctance to engage in direct competition with his father and having a mother who had played Machiavellian games with him clearly set the stage for problems with work, as experienced by another patient. Bill, a thirty-eight-year-old manager of a chain of retail stores, turned down a major promotion that required him to relocate fifty miles from home.

When he rejected the job, Bill thought he'd done the right thing for his family, until the repercussions of his decision hit him. The more he thought about giving up the promotion, the more it haunted him. He felt foolish, then stupid, then a failure. He was stuck, hating himself, for six months. That's when he came to see me.

Bill talked about his parents, describing his mother as overinvested in him, clinging to grandiose expectations of his future success—"She wanted to be a Rose Kennedy, the mother of a President," he said. At the same time, she put his father down, calling him a "real disappointment," although objectively speaking, the man was fairly successful.

What was more trenchant was Bill's example of the many real-life contests and comparisons his mother set up for him with his father, beginning from when he was seven or eight. Wanting to be a worthy opponent for her, he went along with her games, too young and confused to figure out why he felt bad about it all. His growing older didn't stop her. She mailed Bill a general-knowledge test clipped from a newspaper. Accompanying it was a note suggesting that she fully expected him to outperform his father, who'd also taken the test and whose score she included. When I asked him how he felt about this, he said:

> . . . I hated being put on the line again. It was absurd of my mother to send the test, and when I asked her why she did, she played the innocent—that she thought I'd find it interesting, that's all.
> But I know it's about her need to compare me to my father. What surprised me was that as annoyed as it made me, I was also a little intimidated by my father's high score.

At first, Bill put off telling his mother he would *not* take the test, a typically passive-aggressive procrastination. However, his mother continued to nag him about it for two months, until he gave in and outperformed his father by a slight margin.

Bill's self-sabotaged career history and the smoky trail of inhibited ambition curling behind it, is, in part, a reaction against his mother's excessive pride in him. In talking it out, Bill admitted that he'd always found her expectations too high—expectations that pivoted around her wishes for him, rather than around *his* interests. Since he believed he could never meet the standards she set for him, there was no point in his trying. Turning down the promotion was another way of not trying, another way of not competing with his "loser" father who could never measure up.

Bill needs to resolve two problems: (1) to unleash his repressed competitive urges rather than keep them reined in, and (2) to stand up to his mother when she makes such ludicrous and divisive requests in the future. In these resolutions lie hope for him. Only by actually engaging in competition can a passive-aggressive man overcome his fear of it—that is, fear of winning or losing out over other men. Similarly, only by asserting his autonomy can he work through his conflict over dependency.

In *The World According to Garp*, the hero says of his origins, "My father was a Goner. From my mother's point of view, that must have made him very attractive. No strings attached. . . ." John Irving's brilliantly convoluted tale of sex roles, love and loyalty probably hit a few nerves with some passive-aggressive men, like Bill, whose parents relate as if there were "no strings attached."

The dynamics between parents may differ widely, but in general, Bill's story reflects a typical scenario in the early life of many passive-aggressive men: the torn loyalties of a confused boy. Overall, the father is perceived as *not quite there*. This could mean that to the boy the father is fearsome and unapproachable, or inept and inadequate, or absent far too often because of work—depriving him of a male figure to identify with.

His mother looms large, though, and becomes one kind of model for subsequent romantic relationships. The passive-aggressive man later becomes involved with women who are seductive, but dangerous and controlling. He knows their "type." As much as he's attracted to such women, so do they play into his fear of intimacy. He deals with the fear, for example, with stubborn attempts to assert his independence or to turn a cold shoulder at inappropriate times.

Setting up an emotional distance can extend to siblings, too, since brothers and sisters are a source of envy and competition for a passive-aggressive man, even into old age. Already unsure of his parents' feelings for him, he's sensitive to each change that takes place with the arrival of a newborn. According to a passive-aggressive man, his parents were inconsistent in their love. A rival, especially a small, cute, helpless one, presented too great an interference for him.

Most children, male or female, resent the intrusion of another love object and they'll protest in their own way—pressing the advantage of big over small, power over nonpower.

Of course, a *younger* sibling can be equally resentful of the power, opportunities and benefits enjoyed by the older or first-born child.

The problem is not that the passive-aggressive man resents his brothers or sisters, which is quite normal, but that parents most likely didn't let him show his jealousy or anger. Warnings from parents, such as "We didn't raise you to be selfish and mean. Give half that cookie to your brother!" can push a boy into passive-aggression. He can go to extremes and destroy a toy, even one of his own, and blame a sibling, just to get him/her in trouble. Or he'll be totally duplicitous—appearing "sweet" to his brother or sister in front of his parents, but mentally torturing him/her when the grown-ups are out of the room. Eventually, these traits become a way of life.

The young passive-aggressive man who couldn't be open about anger used countless other ways to communicate hostility. He may have been thoroughly destructive, whining and troublesome, all the while hoping to escape punishment. Interestingly, the most common reasons parents bring passive-aggressive sons into therapy are such symptoms as sulkiness, stubbornness, academic underachievement, lack of bladder or bowel control, poor eating habits, excessive sleep, refusing to speak and being accident-prone—*all* acts of rebellion, many of them acted out in school.

Already troubled by how to deal with authority at home, the passive-aggressive youngster has to cope with a second authority figure—the teacher at school. By school age, society has expectations of him and he meets them in his unique way. Some passive-aggressive boys shine at school—it's a place where they find acceptance and acknowledgment through achievement. Others are armed and ready with *feasible* but phony excuses about not doing homework or turning in a special project. ("The electricity was turned off and we had to sit in the dark. . . ." "We had to take my sister to the emergency room. . . .")

He wants to be popular and looked up to by other kids,

but most likely, the young passive-aggressive man finds his notoriety by pulling any number of irritating diversions intended to disrupt the class. He'll ask the teacher pointless questions or answer in a smart-alecky way; he'll make excessively frequent trips to the bathroom, fail to complete his homework or hand in sloppy assignments. Poor performance ends up injuring his self-esteem and perpetuates a vicious circle. Such underachievement evolves later into work inhibition, although many men grow out of it.

ADOLESCENCE: THE TESTING PHASE

Conflict between autonomy and dependency bursts into flames during the heat of adolescence, at best a difficult and ambiguous time. Having outgrown the dependencies of childhood, the adolescent isn't fully able to take on the responsibilities of adulthood. It's a period of confusion, self-testing—a wavering between appropriate and inappropriate behavior. "The law for father and son and mother and daughter," wrote George Bernard Shaw in *Man and Superman*, "is not the law of love; it is the law of revolution, of emancipation, of final supersession of the old and worn-out by the young and capable. . . ." Adolescence is all about emotional shifts, upheavals and coming to terms with oneself and, finally, reuniting with parents in a new way.

Acutely aware of how his freedom is limited, and eager to make his mark on the world, the adolescent is the rebel, notorious for the power struggles he launches with his parents, with teachers, with anyone signifying "authority." "What are you rebelling over?" an intolerant shopkeeper asks a young and jumpy Marlon Brando in *The Wild One*, the classic biker film of youth in search of themselves. "What have you got?" he answers, pleased with himself and his glib wisdom—an answer, in fact, that resonated through Brando's generation and every generation after him. Beyond exercising his will, the adolescent is known for his moodiness, stubbornness and lack of cooperation. Parental words fall on deaf ears.

Parents aren't without feelings, and in their way, they resist the changes taking place with their growing children. What they feel most is *rejection*. Teenagers are pulling away from the dependency of a parental relationship—especially with mothers. There are fewer family-centered activities, less hugging and touching.

The teenager is busy learning how to negotiate the world—to wheel and deal, if only among his friends and potential love interests. During this passage into adulthood, he's finding himself, his *style*, working through the discomforts of growing up; and while it's a time of figuring oneself out, so is it the peak of passive-aggressive behavior. This is *normal*. Unsure of themselves, adolescents will begin using passive-aggression, comfortable with its noncommittal aspects.

For a passive-aggressive man, "normal" phases of adolescence tend to be especially trying. He's conflicted by a compelling need to be defiant—to tell his parents that he's not a child under their thumb—and by a clumsy inability to assert himself directly. He often chooses negativism over outright rebellion. He might feel his parents are too restrictive or unjust, but, emotionally, he doesn't feel powerful enough to challenge them directly. However much he tries to prove his strength, he tends to feel weak, fearing that he doesn't measure up.

Part of this fear of not measuring up comes from the ongoing conflict with his father and what is now a big subject at home: disciplinary problems. Coming from childhood perception of a father as either absent, distant or withdrawn, the adolescent boy defies his father's authority at home, constantly forcing him to reestablish his power. His mother may be on his side in this battle—goading her son to misbehave, or at least silently approving of these confrontations.

Testing himself against his father's authority and experience in the world, sometimes the teenager becomes his mother's unwitting agent, fighting his father on her behalf, goaded on because of *her* anger toward his father. Or his father may manipulate him into being allies, men against women, to avenge any of *his* unexpressed anger. It is understandable if the adolescent ends up confused because he's a pawn in his parents' marriage. Being torn between his parents in this way has another consequence other than confusion: the passive-aggressive man may grow up feeling that he's *not* responsible for his behavior; that someone else pushed him into it and that he has no choice. It's easy to see how fractured family communication leads to indirectness as an adult.

The adolescent passive-aggressive student, like his grade-school equivalent, continues to act out in school. With the greater freedom that comes with age, he may become more impossible: he cuts classes, comes late, takes drugs, falls asleep at his desk and when papers are due he invents stories for not handing them in. If excuses aren't accepted, he becomes self-righteous, feels victimized and maybe even throws a tantrum. And since the passive-aggressive adolescent feels he deserves special treatment, he'll test the limits of a teacher's authority and scope out how flexible he/she is and what he can get away with. His goal is to be as provocative as possible, staying within the bounds of the acceptable.

By the end of adolescence, the passive-aggressive man's personality is fully formed.

MOVING INTO ADULTHOOD

Emotional growth doesn't stop with adolescence but continues throughout life. While our personalities are more or less fully formed by adulthood, certain life events have a significant impact on our personalities. These events or stages of life range from marriage and birth of children, to sudden illness or miraculous cure, career success, just getting by or failure, to death of parents or a spouse or child, to unforeseen events that may erupt any time until we reach retirement and old age.

Of course, adulthood inevitably brings with it the realities of making one's way in the world. It means choosing work that becomes more than just a job and a salary, and selecting a mate who is more than a steady Saturday night date. For the passive-aggressive man still bound up in earlier emotional conflicts, real life brings with it hot-button responses to the key issues of intimacy, dependency, anger and commitment. Any and all of these experiences may potentially increase or decrease the kind of behavior that trips him up.

So let's start with a major source of his problems—*dependency.*

5

RIDING THE DEPENDENCY TREADMILL

THERE'S AN OLD joke about a man who wakes up one morning to find that during the night a storm has toppled a tree across his driveway. He decides to saw it into logs rather than having it hauled away. Although his old hand saw won't do the job, he remembers that a neighbor down the block has a new chain saw that he may be able to borrow.

On his way down the block, the idea of asking his neighbor for a favor begins to rankle: after all, he doesn't know the guy that well. What if the neighbor won't lend him the saw—thinking he's a klutz with power tools, or worse, that he won't *return* it. What kind of neighbor, the man thinks, *is* this guy?

The man works himself up into a state of wild indignation, certain that he'll be turned down. He bangs on his neighbor's front door and when the guy answers he yells, "Okay, so keep your damn chain saw!"

This illustrates a truth we've all lived: we reject people, favors or help in advance because we don't believe our requests will come with an easy (or generous) give-and-take or without conditions that will obligate us. This joke is particularly revealing for understanding passive-aggressive behavior: a passive-aggressive man trips himself up by turning a simple need into an episode of contention. This particular man's train of thought and subsequent outburst pivot around one of the major conflicts in his life—not anger or pride over asking a favor of a stranger, but *dependency*.

A misdirected and emotionally charged dependency fuels the *passive* side of the passive-aggressive man's personality. He's a man who's afraid of being dependent, and confused about how much dependency is too much or too little. Either way, he's angry about it.

The passive-aggressive man may fantasize about being the conquering hero and even get to be "the man in charge," but he'll struggle with feelings of neediness and helplessness. What exactly is he up against when his passive side takes over?

A CLOSE LOOK AT DEPENDENCY

Because we're human, we all depend on others for our material and physical survival (our employers, our landlords, our trust-fund managers, the kindness of strangers, etc.) and for getting our emotional needs met (from our parents, siblings, lovers, spouses, children, friends, colleagues).

Dependency is a characteristic of human existence. Humans go through a naturally longer period of dependency than any other species. While a two-year-old house cat turned out into the wild still has nature and instinct on his side, a two-year-old child has severely limited skills for taking care of himself.

Because the human brain, at birth, is able to do little more than control the most basic instincts for survival, it requires time to develop and fulfill its potential. Until then, we're dependent on caretakers, like mothers and fathers. Sometimes our dependency lasts longer. Take, for example, Cliff Claven, the postman character in the sitcom "Cheers," bound to his mother for thirty-six years and proud of it.

In the previous chapter, I talked about *individuation*—the stage of a child's development when he feels secure in the fact that his mother will be where he left her, even if he wanders out of her sight. At this point in his development he learns that she's not an extension of his body, but a separate individual. Once a child has accepted this key difference between "me" and "not me," he can develop the ability to take care of himself.

How dependent an adult remains on his mother/father/ older sibling/nanny/caretaker hinges on how successfully he works out the tensions and conflicts about separation and individuation. A passive-aggressive man, though, gets stuck here in his conflict over separation and his problems with dependency pervade his whole life. At four years old or forty years old, he feels the same way: scared and insecure if he's not in constant contact with someone important to him. His mind races with internal dialogue that brings him to a pitch before he cools down, making relationships a source of constant anxiety. ("Karen's great . . . really great. But she's always out somewhere. Where is she? Why isn't she answering my messages. Who was that guy she met through work? The lawyer. No, not him. Who cares anyway? I won't bother calling her again. . . .") You can hear how he fights to demonstrate his independence while revealing quite the opposite.

What if he were to recognize how dependent he is? Then things get difficult. His internal dialogue does a 180-degree turn. ("Why is Karen always hovering over me? What's she doing now? It's too quiet. She must be reading. Why's she reading when she promised to go with me to buy a new jacket? She's a drag in stores, anyway. It always winds up costing me a fortune to have her help me do nothing. Women! What the hell!") His resentment spills out. The conflict over dependency churns in him because he hasn't quite accepted its healthy aspect—what I call *mutual dependency*—and so he panics.

Although our survival as adults doesn't depend on someone's constant ministrations, it's natural to be involved with, dependent on and tended to by others. This is true for all of us. You let yourself be cared for and you take care of someone else, willingly assuming either role. Mutual dependency also implies that however enriching another's presence may be in your life, your emotional survival doesn't depend on him or her. Once you can accept this, you can seek out dependency more freely, not out of fear of being alone and needy.

A healthy person selects appropriate people on whom to depend. Living for and through a child and making yourself dependent on him or her, is, for example, an inappropriate choice. But a healthy interchange can exist when you accept the simple truth about feeling dependent, when others accept theirs and you both are willing to meet each other's needs voluntarily and generously.

A bit less healthy about acknowledging dependency, a passive-aggressive man takes a deep breath and runs briskly in the other direction. Dependency makes him feel weak, incompetent and, worst of all, needy. Feeling needy, he fears you'll take advantage of him and that you can't be counted on. The truth is, for the passive-aggressive man to improve his relationships, he needn't become less dependent, but he needs to learn to *accept* dependency as natural. Once he trusts you, he'll see that a relationship is not a volley in ongoing power struggles.

However, there are some battles he's still fighting with his passive side.

THE DEPENDENCY DILEMMA

If anyone automatically (if subconsciously) puts you and others in the role of *authority figure*, it's a passive-aggressive man. It's an emotional reflex that gets him in hot water. Once he's made you important and powerful, he puts himself in the "one down" position, powerless and dependent—and this makes him angry. Feeling inferior, and angry to boot, reinforces his passive-aggression.

What will he then do? Act out and seek power *his* way. He'll procrastinate for months. Or destroy whatever is at his fingertips. Or tell a lie every other sentence to make sure you don't get the information you need. Or, as another way of manifesting his power, he'll withhold his commitment to a relationship. Panic about dependency skews his ability to think rationally. ("What's the point of trying to establish a relationship with this woman if I don't get what I want from her anyhow?")

The passive-aggressive man believes he's surrounded by a world in which he's overly dependent on powerful adults and unable to control his environment. He assumes the role of a child. In his world, outside forces determine his future happiness no matter what he does. He feels he has little or no influence in getting you or anyone else to give him what he wants. He sees you as inconsistent and unpredictable.

In this tightly circumscribed world populated with people more powerful than he, the passive-aggressive man will perceive any request made of him as a reminder of his inadequacy. For him, cooperation is tantamount to submission, knuckling under. It's shaded with dark suggestions of powerlessness and the threatening question: Who's in control? It's either you or he—never both.

So while he may rebel against you ("Don't think you can push *me* around!"), he's the one who has put you in control in the first place. He can then fight against an adversary, and in the end, his passive-aggressive tactics control you. ("Now I've got you!") It's this state of acrimony that he enjoys— and there's the rub. By drawing you into his orbit of perpetual and unresolved conflict, he circles commitment, pushes at trust and challenges his fear of dependency.

He's on the horns of the dependency/passivity dilemma and it throws him, since passive-aggression is never the route to the establishment of a truly secure autonomous identity.

Ruth's experience with Phil is a typical case. A vivacious art director in her early thirties, Ruth told me of the problems she's having with Phil, her boyfriend, a dynamic divorced man in the retail business. She's been dating him regularly for six months; for the first three months, they got along well, if self-consciously. Then they eased more naturally into each other's lives and things changed. A new pattern slowly emerged. Ruth would stay with Phil on weekends, but when she left on Sundays she would feel that when she closed the door she would never see him again.

Ruth said:

> We can have a really good time together on Saturday and a romantic night of love-making, then he'll wake up Sunday and behave as if I'm a huge intrusion. He wants me there, then he doesn't. He tells me how monogamous he is, then how he's a "loner."
>
> Suddenly we have nothing to say to each other. He'll make a phone call, set up an appointment and look like the cat who ate the mouse. If I ask who he was talking to he says, "it's personal." He makes me feel insecure.
>
> We wind up sniping at each other and it gets around to why we're with each other. I ask him if he wants to separate for a while. This gets him crazy and he accuses me of dating someone behind his back . . . and we're off.
>
> We fight. I leave. He calls me two or three days later, speaking in double-talk about what happened and asking me if I'll be over at his house on Friday night, as usual. And so it goes.

It's interesting to note that Phil, playing his game of catch-me-if-you-can, didn't reveal any of his inner self until he had Ruth hooked. Over the first three months, Ruth felt their self-consciousness had to do with finding each other's boundaries—emotionally, socially, philosophically and so on. Whatever anxiety Phil harbored about his growing sense of dependency on Ruth was hidden beneath a cool exterior.

The concealed inner man struck out at Ruth just at the moment he knew in his heart how much he needed her—when she was about to leave, on Sundays. He protected himself from this realization by perpetuating and stirring up doubt (hers) and conflicts (hers, too). His fears about trust seeped out every Sunday because Saturday's emotions were too intense for him. To acknowledge the depth of his feelings, he thought, would give her control over his life. Instead, he struck out by pushing her away—angry that she stirred his feelings, anticipating that she would probably leave him. To make it easier on himself, he had to establish his stronghold and reject *her*.

Phil plays out this drama of dependency/autonomy, swinging between obedient dependency and defiant resistance. He's like the donkey who vacillates one way and then another, unable to decide which bale of hay is better. And like the indecisive donkey, he starves to death.

Since Ruth cares about Phil and wants the intimacy to continue, she falls for his weekend ploy—love, warmth, cooldown, meltdown, damage control. Unfortunately, he's wasting time and hurting feelings, beating up himself, and Ruth, for nothing.

A passive-aggressive man shows signs of his underlying conflict over dependency in a number of other classic ways.

FEAR OF AUTONOMY

The passive-aggressive man seeks acceptance by others before he can accept himself. In fact, some may look to others to help them frame an authentic sense of self. ("Who am I?/*You* tell me.") It's the strength of others' judgments about him— that he's smart, that he's affable, that he's reliable, that he's a good enough son and a father who tries—that gives him direction and ego. On the one hand, he seeks acceptance, which he hopes will lead to love and respect by those who confer it on him; on the other hand, he resents his dependency on them to his very soul. What happens is that his *passivity* often elicits the response he seeks (an answer), which he then throws back. ("Who are *you* to tell me who I am?")

Roger, a patient of mine who's strongly passive-aggressive, related a dream that suggests this very pattern. In the dream, Roger put on two coats, one over the other, and his wife caught him "in the act" of layering them. The inside coat was a "ratty" old windbreaker that his wife disliked, and over it was a classic but basically nondescript topcoat, an "organization man" tailored affair, gray and conservative.

The dream is a vivid one. It exemplifies the contrast between Roger's bland, conformist exterior and his wilder, more nonconformist interior—the difference between how he appears on the surface and what churns below. The neurotic conflict in the dream is not just this contrast between the two sides of Roger's personality, but how careless he was about concealing his rebelliousness from his wife. The hidden coat told me that Roger wants to fight authority, but is afraid to stand up to it. However, as with most passive-aggressive men, Roger couldn't resist calling attention to this "bad boy" side. It's part of that ambivalence—wanting to be upright and "good" (his passive side) and needing to assert himself or defy authority (his aggressive side).

As long as Roger depends on the approval of others and holds the conformist banner, he squelches who he really might become; by the same token, as long as he seeks out power struggles for no reason at all, he'll never get what he wants.

LACK OF INITIATIVE

When faced with challenges, opportunities or conflicts, the more passive breed of passive-aggressive man plays a waiting game: he waits for others to solve his problems, for his luck to change or for someone to rescue him. Since he believes change comes from outside forces, not internal decisions and fortitude, it stands to reason he also believes that all he has to do is show up. Help will come.

If you are so inclined, you see in his neediness fertile fields to harvest: you want to straighten him out, give his life structure and help him through tough times. You fall for his potential and ignore signs of his very fundamental personality problems. You may even have a clearer picture of where he's headed than he has. But there's a catch.

If his life appears open-ended, it's because he doesn't effectively organize, sort out, take action and resolve problems. The passive-aggressive man waits for you to initiate action—whereupon he feels controlled by you. Lack of initiative indicates another kind of conflict over dependency. It reveals a preference for and comfort with the status quo.

No matter how troubled relationships get, the passive-aggressive man will not unilaterally leave them. Unlike most people, the passive-aggressive man accepts layer upon layer of emotional clutter from interpersonal strife: "I like things complicated," he'll say by way of explanation, as if such a statement implies he has constructed a fascinating life of depth with order and variety. Instead, he's taken up residence in the familiarity of his discontented chaos.

The passive-aggressive man prefers to stay aboard, half off and half on. If he wants out, he'll engineer the situation so you are forced to break up with him. Leaving is too *real*, too actively self-assertive, requiring too much initiative. It would allow you to actually blame him, something he doesn't like at all. A passive-aggressive man wants *you* to take responsibility for the downfall of the relationship. This gives him the opportunity to feel sorry for himself and make you feel guilty for leaving him.

Rescuers especially are moved to help him—and in the beginning, he loves the attention and fantasies of what the "rescue" will do for him. It may be as important as his getting you to do his work for him or as minor as offering suggestions regarding how he might accomplish a goal. Your efforts will probably go unappreciated, since his fault-finding and negativism can triumph over anyone's best intentions and commonsense advice. ("Yes, but . . .") This, of course, is his goal—to resist you. He turns your own energies back against you. He resents needing your help, and because he does, he may even take pleasure in explaining how inadequate you've been.

The passive-aggressive man's lack of initiative actually belies a fear of rejection. Martin, a twenty-four-year-old passive-aggressive man, came into treatment with me because he had great difficulty maintaining friendships and romantic relationships. He had a real inaptitude for warming to people. While Martin knew he made a good first impression, he assumed that people, especially women, wouldn't like him once they got to know him better. When he came into treatment, he was so demoralized that although he desperately wanted to have friendships, he made no genuine efforts in that direction. In fact, Martin actively pushed people away.

Anticipating inevitable rejection, he acted elusive and cool, implying he did women a favor by going out with them. Of course, the opposite was true. It was the offensive/defensive approach to winning affection, and hopefully, love. It's the self-defeating ploy again ("I don't need you") covering dependency needs. Unfortunately, the more distant he was, the less chance he had of getting what he wanted. The therapy centered on making Martin vulnerable to the risk of rejection and disappointment—possible dangers on the only road to establishing relationships.

When I suggested that Martin take the initiative, his response was, "What's the point? She'll never like me anyway." In Martin's case, as with some passive-aggressive men, hopelessness wins out over taking the challenge and trying new opportunities. And when there are no opportunities, because of his sabotaging them, he then blames fate. And by blaming fate, or powers on high, he reluctantly accepts his passivity.

This pessimism applies equally as much to the passive-aggressive man's work life as to his social life. On the job, the passive-aggressive man focuses his attention on why things *can't* get accomplished, rather than how they *can*. The capacity to imagine constructive solutions to problems appears to be missing from his makeup.

JoAnne, a patient, has watched her brother suffer from this problem all his life. George bought a partnership in a video/record store, but he has a poor sense of management and a distorted sense of priorities. The mistake JoAnne made was to invest in the business. The shop is always low on stock or short of help—George has a hard time even relying on employees. JoAnne told me:

George has friends smarter than him in business, but either he won't ask their advice or won't take it. It's a sign of defeat for him. It's crazy!

As things have gotten worse and worse, George gets more and more panicky. Then he's *lost*. Rather than get back on track, he gives up in frustration. He's done it a million times with jobs. I loaned him the money for the shop, hoping George would shape up. But apparently not!

What is more destructive, George doesn't learn from his mistakes. He attributes his failure to irrelevant or minor obstacles: "People push me too hard," or "The market is bad for small businesses," or "Sure, right. Everyone's got advice but no real experience in *my* business," or "I can't concentrate." It's a pessimistic attitude that takes away responsibility for the failure, and justifies his reluctance to ask others for help. If things look hopeless, why continue? If something is out of his control, what's the point of trying?

SINS OF OMISSION

The paradox of dependency (or passivity) and hostility (or aggression) showing themselves *at the same time* comes alive with "sins of omission." When a passive-aggressive man refuses to give you what you want or need (attention, affection, assistance, a loan) consider it a skewed, *but to him real*, manifestation of hostility.

It means to him that he doesn't have to jump to please you, he doesn't have to show his concern for you and most of all he doesn't have to treat you as someone with real dependency needs of your own. He resists you, rejects you . . . and you're often unsure why. He leaves you out in the cold, your needs unattended to, your feelings hurt.

In a time of need the passive-aggressive man is, as the saying goes, "an hour late, a dollar short or a block away." You may be counting on him, but chances are he will disappoint you. "Sins of omission" make the passive-aggressive man who he is as much as does his fear of intimacy: he backs off at the moment of truth, doing nothing when he should be doing something.

When someone hides behind a veil of innocence and good intentions, it is difficult to hold him responsible for problems resulting from an omission. (He "meant to be there to help you move," but he told you his back tends to give out, so he couldn't help it if you were waiting for him. . . .)

This is what makes the passive-aggressive man's hostility so slippery. Every time you think you've been mistreated, he can give you a dozen reasons why that's not the case. He's not in the slightest bit like the person who throws a brick through the window, or insults you to your face, or cheats you in business. Sins of commission are more obvious and cannot be denied, but sins of omission are equally hurtful.

One patient, Laura, had a boyfriend who habitually "forgot" things: pick up food for dinner, buy her a birthday present, do the dishes. As with many sins of omission, she was reluctant to challenge him, until I suggested she substitute the words "didn't want to" each time he said he "forgot" something. Right away, she felt more entitled to be mad about it, and had the strength to confront him. Everyone wants and needs things from other people, and you have a right to be angry when you're disappointed.

FINDING A BALANCE

The question women ask me most often about the passive-aggressive man's dependency conflict is: How can I get him to make a change in a pattern as old as he is? How can I instill in him a sense of trust? When will he voluntarily give me what he knows I want?

The answer is to find a balance between encouraging his sense of power, independence and choice and supporting him when he feels weak and dependent.

One simple but effective method of increasing the passive-aggressive man's sense of independence is to *remind him that he has a range of options from which to choose*, that you're not forcing him or telling him what he *must* do. He's a grown-up running his own life, with the capacity for intimacy, and capable of success. He may have forgotten that he has this freedom and power.

These are ongoing themes in getting the passive-aggressive man on a healthier psychological track—reminders and choices. And although there are consequences to the choices he makes—good and bad—he needs to understand that they're still *his* decisions. The decisions he makes and the actions he takes have predictable consequences and effects. The fact that there are choices helps him feel he has control over his destiny—he will see that he's more than an angry or wounded creature. Choice, by definition, will empower him to take action and *make changes*. This helps him put things into clearer perspective.

If he feels too dependent and powerless in a relationship (and this includes ones at work and home; with relatives, friends or colleagues) you can help him establish autonomy by pointing out how he has control over many sectors of his life. Be specific. ("You're in charge of your department. . . ." "Your friends usually rely on your opinion. . . ." "The kids look up to you. . . .")

Remember, however helpless he is, you're not his mother. Don't fall into his trap of playing that role. Making decisions for him only sets you up for criticism and complaint. As you help him to break his dependency habit, expect him to try to undermine your efforts. If you choose a movie or the restaurant because he's deferred to you ("You pick. I'm open."), he could respond with: "You know how I hate foreign films and reading subtitles. . . ." or "How like you to pick a restaurant this far from the office and this expensive. . . ." The most effective way to counteract this gambit is to put the responsibility back on his shoulders. Tell him, "*You're* the one who feels strongly about this (deal, movie, neighborhood, bill paying, etc.), so *you* decide." He may put off making a choice, and the delays may try your patience, but there are no shortcuts.

If you're a woman who tends to be a Rescuer (which gives him an out—you're masterful at taking charge) or a Manager (the woman who has a hard time taking no for an answer), *step back*. Give him the power of choice. He may play the waiting game, and if you're assertive and impatient, you'll have a hard time sitting around while he does nothing. But remember, he's got to be the one to make the choice to feel empowered. And once he's agreed to make the choice, be on his side when he does. The payoff is worth it. The more empowered he feels, the less passive-aggressive he'll be.

A CLOSING NOTE

As the passive-aggressive man comes to grips with who he is in the scheme of things—and realizes that he's not powerless or ineffective and is still a man even if he makes mistakes—it means he's defusing his dependency conflicts. Needing others doesn't have to mean he's beholden to them or that they control him. Mutual and comfortable dependency is a goal worth working toward, in any arena—professionally, in the family or among friends.

Now let's look at the flip side of passivity—aggression and anger—and how the passive-aggressive man deals with it.

6

FACING THE DRAGON: THE PASSIVE-AGGRESSIVE MAN AND ANGER

"WHY CAN'T HE admit he's angry?"

"I wish he'd come out swinging—it's better than trying to fight with someone who pretends he's not mad!"

"The man can smile at me like nothing's wrong, then a minute later demolish me—but I don't know what I've done!"

"I wish he'd scream—just once!"

When you're involved with a passive-aggressive man, it's likely that you've made these same remarks. As with other hot-button feelings like dependency, a passive-aggressive man doesn't easily own up to *anger*. This is what makes him so confusing to deal with. Life would be so much easier if only you understood when and why he's angry. And it's far from easy to interpret his oddball denial games. So the question is: How do you get this guy to acknowledge his grievances, to get them out in the open so that you can deal with them? Is there a trick to getting him to take responsibility for his anger, and if and when he does, what should you do then? Let's start with how he deals with anger.

SUBMERGED HOSTILITY: HOW IT PLAYS OUT

Does the following sound familiar? He calls you, speaks four or five seconds, then puts you on hold for four or five minutes; he asks why you're wearing that dress again when you know it's so unflattering on you; he shows up forty-five minutes late for a dinner party with your parents; he tells you a friend doesn't like the way you redecorated the living room, but *he* likes it just fine. If the passive-aggressive man is consistent about anything, it's his talent for communicating hostility. He may think he's being an expert, a critic, a busy man, *but what he's really being is angry.*

Anger is at the core of passive-aggression, even when it is denied, submerged or called something else. But however much he may try to disguise it, his anger is never entirely concealed, since for him to fully hide his anger would be to miss the point. He needs to call attention to it. For this reason, we speak of passive-aggression as anger with a hook—aggression mixed with dependency.

Many passive-aggressive men will sulk rather than raise their voices, explode in rage or come clean about what's bothering them. Those who are more demonstrative may let you know by tormenting, phone-slamming gestures that they're angry, but they aren't generous with the specific reasons *why*. Passive-aggressive guys contain their anger, but their message ("I'm angry and it's your fault") comes through loud and clear.

When he does fight openly, his style is more of the boxer who'll go at you with irritating jabs to the belly, hoping to sap your strength before you can throw your knockout blow.

Psychoanalyst Willard Gaylin, in *The Rage Within*, compared the effect of the passive-aggressive man's fighting style to the Tar Baby of the Uncle Remus children's stories, who gets you so mad that you throw a punch, but, to your surprise, your fist *sticks* to him. Pummel him and he absorbs your blows as if nothing was going on. Eventually, you give up in exhaustion, fury or tears. The Tar Baby wins the fight, *not* by returning your blows, but by using the force of your own anger and strength against you.

The passive-aggressive man, though, is no warrior. Like the gummy Tar Baby, he makes you angry at him, but when you show it, he's stricken. Remind him that it's four months past deadline for a contract to be drawn up and listen to what he says. ("How could you accuse me of not getting the contract done on time? I've got all the materials right here on my desk. No one works harder than me.") Such comments are meant to deflect your attention and possibly to arouse your guilt. Or say he promised to help you move the furniture, since the painters were coming the next day, but he fails to show up. Then he calls at midnight, saying, "Why don't you calm down? I didn't call sooner because you said you needed more time to yourself . . . to fix the place up. Remember?"

When people fight, they want to know that the other person will respond, defend him or herself in terms of the real issues and be willing to bring the conflict to some resolution. The passive-aggressive man passively absorbs your blows, even depriving you of the pleasure of having landed a few. If he responds at all, it's with the rabbit punch—off the subject, sarcastic, pointless. His victory, albeit a Pyrrhic one, is the means by which he creates his victimhood out of the situation—you strike out, not with your fists, but by pointing to his inappropriate behavior, and how it hurts you. When he doesn't respond, your frustration rises and you show your irritation. It may even escalate into full-fledged rage. This is the passive-aggressive man's game—to work you into a lather, confirming his impression of you as dangerous and overbearing, someone not to be trusted, and he becomes the "innocent" wounded party.

Norman, one passive-aggressive man I know, says with great self-pity, "What have I done wrong now?" He feels no remorse for how he's treated others—all he sees is that people are angry at him. He doesn't see why! It seems inconceivable that someone doesn't know that if he treats people badly, they won't like him. But Norman will tell you that you have been arbitrary or demanding ("If only you understood. . . .")

The passive-aggressive man tends to feel embattled and resentful as he hunkers down, preparing to absorb your attack. Since he always expects to be attacked, when you do something constructive like airing a simple grievance, he experiences it as an assault. You can see it on his face—he can't trust you. And you feel guilty, since that's not what you intended at all. Cynthia, a patient, told me:

> When I mention the simplest complaint to my boyfriend, he gets this look, as if he'd done something hideously wrong. It's a puppy-dog look that makes me feel like I've wounded him or something. Next thing I know, I'm apologizing to him, and he's never heard my complaint, much less responded to it.

It's a fascinating study in a kind of self-involvement: the passive-aggressive man experiences his own hostility only through the negative reactions of others—which, of course, he perceives as unfair criticism. Why should he be held accountable? It's demeaning. Give me a break, get off my back—these are his refrains. Since he doesn't understand his motives, he is caught in this childish bind.

Unfortunately, his resentment spills over, and since he will not acknowledge it, there is no basis for dealing with it. It is difficult to say, "All right, I'm angry because you did this. . . ." when he is unable to respond honestly, "I did *that*, and it happens too frequently. . . ." Then both of you are unable to finish with, "I regret I upset you, and here's what I think we can do. . . ." What happens instead is a chain reaction of other problems: evasiveness, confusion, prolonging bad feelings, counterproductive behavior, and great dissatisfaction with the relationship.

DEALING WITH ANGER

The trick to dealing with submerged hostility is to bring it out into the open. Your hardest job will be to convince the passive-aggressive man in your life that *it's okay to be angry* so he can own up to how he feels. What you do and how you decide to respond has a major impact on whether or not he will feel comfortable enough to express his anger in appropriate ways. Since anger is such a hot topic for all of us— it may frighten, embarrass or confuse us—we may unintentionally discourage its direct expression. The message comes through: it is not acceptable for him to be angry; we don't want to hear about it; we don't want to deal with it.

Worse yet is the impulse to retaliate. To be upset is to lose one's thread of reason and become less clearheaded than one would like to be. It's the difference between saying what you mean ("When you keep interrupting me, I can't tell you what you need to know") or retaliating with sarcasm and outright hostility. ("Here you go again—I don't know why I bother talking to you at all!") This is the very type of response that stops conversations or arguments dead. It will escalate problems with the passive-aggressive man, not diminish them.

In *Anger: The Misunderstood Emotion*, author Carol Tavris writes, "verbal aggression usually fails because it riles up the other person and makes him or her inclined to strike back, whereas a description of your state of mind constitutes less of an attack, inspiring the other person to make amends." When you encourage openness—that is, uncover the reason you feel angry in the first place—you're bound to make a better case for yourself. This "feelings report" approach definitely has a better chance of working, especially with a passive-aggressive man.

Some women try the exact opposite way of coping with anger. More comfortable with a passive-aggressive man's inclination to deny anger, they quickly try to humor him out of it. ("Oh, Charlie, forget about it . . . what does it really matter? You're too good to let this get to you.") For them, choosing the path of least resistance brings some comfort. However obnoxious and infuriating the guy's sulking may be, *passive*-aggression is safer for them than *direct* aggression.

The man who's humored out of anger that he may or may

not have otherwise expressed doesn't necessarily feel better, or less angry—he just stews. To make matters worse, he'll interpret your attempts (and your jokes) as *stifling*, or controlling. On the one hand, he's easily intimidated and afraid of confrontation, and on the other hand, he resents the condescension implicit in your attempts to "handle" his anger.

Suppressing anger isn't constructive nor is it an airtight solution, even with good humor snapping the lid closed. You may find that humoring him is preferable in the short run, but over the long run, it has insidious effects on the relationship. Make no mistake about it, a passive-aggressive man's anger will come out in other ways, inevitably, passive-aggressively. So, in general, I recommend the "feelings report" approach for both of you. It avoids the twin dangers of suppression and retaliation. But to use this approach you must feel comfortable dealing with anger, unlike a recent patient of mine.

Debra loved her copywriting job at an up-and-coming advertising agency, but she clashed with Roger, an ambitious colleague of thirty-five who'd been at the agency a year longer than she. Exceptionally sharp at spotting people's quirks and behavior patterns, Debra described Roger in classic passive-aggressive terms ("manipulative, control freak, evasive, low frustration level for not getting his way, overly self-protective, overreacting and attacking"). Roger couldn't take the mildest criticism, and he'd punish Debra by sulking for days on end. This would just make her furious. ("I can't work with someone who behaves like I don't exist. And sometimes I don't even know what I've done to offend him.")

She was caught in a frustrating cycle. She was openly pushing for a promotion, edging into Roger's turf, and consequently had become a thorn in his side. A master at the indirect insult, Roger tried to undermine her confidence. At meetings, for example, he'd level a cool glance at her and say, with a charming lilt in his voice, "Don't you think the meeting is too crowded, Debra?" implying that she was extraneous. Often, he told her lies that made no sense for him to tell and that were easy enough for her to check on.

Debra was disturbed by the way Roger was treating her, and didn't know how to respond. When she told me that she'd prefer Roger to get his anger out in the open and over with rather than play passive-aggressive games, I challenged her. I asked her to imagine what such an interaction would be like. When she described this hypothetical scene with actual flares of temper, Debra saw that dealing directly with anger was *not* appealing to her either: she discovered the extent to which fear of anger limited her actions.

Debra no more wanted Roger to express his anger openly than she wanted him to express it indirectly. What Debra actually wanted was for Roger to be *less* angry with her (and less threatened by her), something entirely different and quite unrealistic. Basically, she wished she didn't have to deal with his anger at all. She then acknowledged that on occasion Roger would begin to vent his anger, and scared of him, she would stop it. Passive-aggression *felt* safer to her than direct aggression. For all Debra's psychological sophistication and sensitivity, she unintentionally pushed Roger in a passive-aggressive direction. My advice: allow him to be more direct. The remainder of the therapy focused on how she could have the courage to face up to other people's anger.

The first breakthrough with a passive-aggressive man is to take a noncritical stance with him. This may succeed in changing his expectations and perception of you. A noncritical stance shows him you accept him for who he is—angry or not. The more you accept him *and he knows it*, the easier it will be to finally reach the point where you can tell him, without rancor, that it's time to drop the subject and move on. As his experience of you changes and he feels more sure of himself, he'll learn to hear criticism of his behavior without interpreting it as criticism of himself.

PROTECTING YOURSELF

A man is entitled to his feelings, but he has no right to vent his rage without concern for the consequences—you're not a punching bag, exposed and unflinching, ready to absorb countless blows.

At times, remember, the anger you're bearing may not have anything to do with you. A man who's angry with his boss may take it out on you when he gets home. Should you encourage such inappropriate anger? Certainly not. Abusing you can't possibly lead to a productive resolution with his boss. In fact, playing it out on you diminishes the likelihood that he *will* confront his boss, a far more constructive move.

The cathartic let-it-all-hang-out approach to resolving anger is overly simplistic. During the late 1960s to the mid-1970s, there were a number of new-age therapies that focused on "getting in touch with your feelings." Anger, the most explosive emotion, was often the most exploited.

Participants in such one-on-one private therapies or in marathon group sessions were asked to voluntarily become angry, working themselves up to full ventilation, often by using an acting technique or two. One system operated by a group member saying again and again to the whole group (or therapist), "*I am angry . . . I am angry . . . I am angry,*" increasing the pitch, summoning an anger-producing memory and "letting it out," with the purpose of unblocking the psyche, thereby moving toward mental health.

Some therapies provided a "bat and ball" approach to ventilating anger. Beating out your rage by striking a pillow or padded equipment was considered a safer, less bloody way of getting back at people who you felt had hurt you.

Will you feel better after screaming in the air or punching a bag? Possibly. But will it help or change your problem? Probably not. We can *manufacture unlimited quantities of anger*, and unless we get to the cause of the problem and fix it, venting is not a solution.

Ultimately, with a passive-aggressive man, your solution is to find the fine line between *setting limits* on his anger to protect yourself, and squelching anger, as Debra did with Bob and Roger. You'll have to rely on your own judgment and sensitivity as to how far to let him go.

What should guide you in finding this fine line is an understanding of the passive-aggressive man's psychological dynamics. His anger, submerged or not, is tied to fear; but there are two kinds of fear. First is the *fear of being hurt by you*. Thus, your retaliation plays into this dynamic, further fueling his anger and passive-aggression. The second dynamic is his *fear of hurting you*, and letting a passive-aggressive man wantonly vent his anger on you in a way that hurts you will only damage the relationship and convince him that his anger really is destructive. Thus, setting limits on his hostile behavior and protecting yourself will make him feel less afraid.

The benefit of the "feelings report" approach is that he'll see that his anger doesn't always do damage and that, in fact, it can lead to constructive results when expressed openly and tactfully. Letting off steam makes sense for both of you, as long as it is done appropriately.

CONFRONTING HIM WITHOUT HEATING THINGS UP

Some problems require that you move straight on course or they are not resolved. You're entitled to your feelings and you've simply got to confront the guy—face him and call his attention to the impact of his behavior: "*This* hurts . . . *that* offends me. When you did *this*, I felt *that*. . . ." Confrontation should refer to specific behaviors, rather than be a criticism of his whole character. Behaviors change; character won't. Thus, for example, if you have a regular tennis game with a friend who frequently comes late or cancels at the last minute, you might choose to discontinue the tennis arrangements rather than break off the friendship.

Confrontation has a twofold purpose. For one, it can increase a passive-aggressive man's insight into the consequences of his actions, which will help him decide how to behave in the future, and two, failing that, it's at least an opportunity to talk to him in a more straightforward manner and extricate yourself from his passive-aggressive mind-bending twists of logic.

There is no need to protect your passive-aggressive spouse/ boyfriend/father/brother/boss from your feelings. If he hurts you, let him know about it. Don't fall into the role of the Victim. The biggest mistake you can make is to let your guilt about "nagging" or "annoying" him with your grievances interfere with your right to face him. Nor should you apologize to him and supply him with an "out" as in this example:

"I'm sorry to bring this up when I know you're so busy, Harry, but I really feel excluded around here, if you know what I mean." You can bet he'll respond to the following words, *"sorry," "busy," "Harry,"* and *"you know,"* brush you off, pick up the phone and make a call rather than hear you out. Instead, make your feelings the subject of your confrontation. Suggest that he's a basically good guy rather than pointing out his flaws or the weight of his obligations. If you want to make headway with him, the following dialogue will probably get you his ear:

"Harry, you've always been fair and I could always count on you. I'm worried about what's happening between us/ what's happening in this department/how I'm being treated. Let's talk it out later over lunch. This is important to me."

You can begin to defuse the power of passive-aggression by tactful confrontation. The face-off can help you square things, eventually defuse hostilities, and allow you to reach a resolution. Be level-headed—wild threats and recriminations are rarely effective and will only put him on the defensive. If you say, "You get one more chance to tell the truth or you'll be sorry. I may not be here in the morning," expect him to say, "Fine!" But unless that's the desired result, you should choose another approach.

Confronting a passive-aggressive man with the consequences of his behavior is a necessary condition for living (and working) with him. Be selective about the issues you bring up and the times you choose to take your stand. Pick your fights. Find nonthreatening ways to reach him; for example, in a letter that he can read in a neutral setting. He can't hear if he feels attacked—he can only attack back. Confront him when he's most likely to absorb what you have to say, and only point out the behavior that most disturbs you. There will also be times when you shouldn't respond at all. Learn to let some things roll off your back.

FIGHTING FAIRLY

Anger is an inherent component of all human relationships, especially romantic ones. The more dependent on someone and vulnerable you feel, the more likely they'll be the object of your hostility as well as your affection. Given the inevitability of anger in all relationships, the question is not whether to express it, but what is the *best* way to clear the air? The long-term success of a relationship depends on finding appropriate channels for expressing and dealing with each other's anger.

Fighting in a relationship is about intimacy and dependency—to be intimate, you must reveal yourself, good and bad. To be intimate, you must come to terms with how much you need the other. As the stakes rise, anger won't be far behind. Fighting is one way, among many, to make a connection with another human being.

Free expression of anger is a testament to the strength of a relationship, not to its fragility. Relationships that don't acknowledge or permit anger are much more brittle and self-conscious. It indicates that neither person has the confidence that the relationship can handle it. In fact, the healthiest relationships can and do handle anger and aggression. Instead of fearing anger, set ground rules for letting it out, and consequently, for making it a constructive force in the relationship.

People in healthy relationships fight just as much as people in unhealthy ones, but the difference is that the healthier ones fight fairly. When there are implicit ground rules, you both begin psychologically, in a way, on equal footing. You respect each other's position, feel you and he are entitled to it, and do your best to find a solution to the problem—the source of the anger. When both of you are concerned, sincere and equally involved, you both have as much to lose and as much to gain. There are no exploitative tactics, low blows or intimidation, personal attacks or diversionary ploys. The basis of a fair fight is to hear the other person out and then respond in turn.

The problem with the passive-aggressive man is that the fair fight is not part of his repertoire. He's used to other behavior—clouding issues, sulking or sarcasm. He won't clarify what's bothering him, and he sometimes is itching to pick a fight for no reason at all. Wives, girlfriends, low-level employees and children are convenient targets.

A passive-aggressive man doesn't see compromise as a mutual win; the "fight" for him is one-sided (his win or else). If he has to make the slightest compromise, he views it as a huge concession for which you should be grateful or guilty. ("I called you, but you weren't in. You ask me to call, and then you're not there.") When you make all sorts of compromises, he takes it for granted. ("I'm working late tonight. We'll have to have dinner about ten . . . ten-thirty. You can wait for me and then we'll order in.")

Fighting with the passive-aggressive man is particularly tiresome because he's always telling you how he's been victimized. Say he's promised to introduce your friend to an important contact but hasn't come through for six months. You ask again, and he says, "I can't think about Toby's career today, and I didn't exactly *promise* I'd get her an interview with Higgins. I have my own problems. I work hard to put two children through private school, and I've done pretty well for you, so give me a break. I have to make an important call and I'm late."

With such an emotionally loaded response, he raises extraneous points that make you feel either mad or guilty about your request. He turns the tables, and the subject changes from how he's procrastinated about helping Toby to how he thinks you devalue him as a provider. Then you are off defending yourself, assuring him he's a success.

Another ploy to get you off the subject and sabotage the fair fight is the empty apology. "I'm sorry. I didn't mean to do it," may stop an argument short, but it's usually meaningless. First, you tell him what's bothering you, and after shifting his position a few times, he may hit his anxiety threshold and simply apologize. It's just a way to get you off the subject, or, as he says, to get you off his back.

You'll know if his apology means anything by how he follows up: Does he change his behavior? Did he make the call for you? Has he stopped the lies? Is he at least making an effort, even if he trips up once in a while?

Because of who he is, there is no such thing as a fair fight with the passive-aggressive man the first time out. As you assert your strength, he automatically will feel weak and taken advantage of. That the balance of power seems to be tipping in your favor will scare him. You'll have to keep at it and develop a basis of trust to prove to him that you won't take advantage of his vulnerability. He needs your help in learning that he can face troubles and conflict and has both dignity and power.

The next step in the fair fight is for you to bring him back to the subject—and he'll stray from it. As he tries to deflect your comments, the key is to keep your focus and reiterate your points. To do this, you must feel entitled to work through the issue. If you're easily intimidated by the dust he kicks up, you'll never get to the issues that bother you, nor will he ever honor your feelings.

Since he's supersensitive to criticism, call attention to the problem between you tactfully, not as a cudgel in the battle. Remember, there is a voice resonating in his unconscious: his mother's. Argument turns up the inner noises, and you may be suddenly interchangeable with a memory. You have to communicate to him, implicitly or explicitly, the following message: "I care about what happens to you and I love you, but I'm not your mother. If you feel that women control you, be aware that I'm not doing this or saying this to be her.

You've got the wrong person. If you want me to treat you like your mother did, find someone else. What we have here is a mutual relationship."

The classic passive-aggressive man may keep pushing you into the Medea role—the mother who would devour her young, or its variation, the bitch goddess. The biggest mistake is to let him manipulate you into assuming such a role. In some cases, it's merely pointing out that he's acting childishly that sets off the transference from you to his mother. When this happens, forget about fair fighting: he's caught in childhood. Don't let him treat you as if you were a domineering figure merely because you want to get to the bottom of your disagreements and make things right again.

MAKING UP

Once the fair fight has reached its peak, the cool-down follows. You probably know from experience that your boyfriend/husband/ father/brother/boss rarely takes the first step toward making up. But don't let the Mexican standoff go on forever. Grab the banner and start the crusade: making up is usually up to you.

Many passive-aggressive men do grow up and change. David had been in therapy with me for two years. He was a twenty-eight-year-old graphic artist living at home with his younger sister, Anne, and their widowed father.

One evening, David came home looking for a fight. He found it on the hall table: a bill that Anne was to have paid. David stormed into her bedroom, where Anne was changing the linen, wielding as a weapon the one subject guaranteed to cause trouble between them: *money.* They often fought about who contributed more to the household. David's penchant for extravagant designer suits, a habit that forced him to borrow money from their father, heightened their arguments, which usually revolved around who was greedy and who was responsible.

David told me:

> When I mentioned the electric bill, Anne said in a nasty tone, "It's not your problem." I said, "You're the one who insists on paying all the bills. I paid them just fine before you took over. Why the hell can't I count on you to do something even a seven-year-old can do?"
>
> We then started at each other with insults about who earns what and who should be doing what. She lost her temper, went into my room, picked up a pile of bills and magazines and threw it at me, scattering the stuff all over the hall, and stormed out.

Anne was the one who wound up looking bad; David came up the innocent party.

David felt vindicated, but he also felt lousy about what he'd done, and he began to see the pattern of passive-aggressive behavior we'd been talking about in therapy. Ignoring the mess Anne had made, he lay down on his bed and turned on the television. An hour or two passed and neither of them said a word, though their father made a crack to Anne about picking up the mess, half siding with David, but not quite.

David admitted that he took a guilty pleasure in the bind he had put Anne in. At some point, she'd have to step into his turf, the hall and entrance to his bedroom, and clean up the mess. He also knew she was seething and wouldn't make the first move. He worried that if he apologized, she'd start another fight and reject him. Finally he faced her:

> "Before we get into another argument about the bill, I want to apologize for picking a fight. Money isn't the issue. It's about Sarah. I have a terrible feeling she wants to break up with me . . . plus I want to move out into my own place and I'm worried about leaving you with all the responsibility for Dad . . . plus things are boiling at work."
>
> Once Anne heard what was going on with me, everything changed. We both got down on our hands and knees, and picked up the papers together.

When Anne understood the source of David's anxiety and the reason for the fight, she stopped being angry and offered her support. They were on the same side again.

As with David, surface hostilities are almost never the real issues in a skirmish with a passive-aggressive man. If you both can discuss the real issues openly and supportively, then the need for passive-aggression will dissipate. This anecdote also shows that a passive-aggressive man *can* face a tough emotional issue, recognize the weakness in how he expresses it and initiate a reconciliation.

If he comes to realize that speaking openly about his concerns—giving a "feelings report"—will *decrease* tension, he will come to trust that doing so will lead to positive results. The passive-aggressive man will always act in his best interest. The trick is to teach him that what's in his best interest will be good for you as well.

Anger and aggression are natural to everyone. To be less angry is not the answer. For someone you care about to accept your anger, even if they disagree, *is* the solution.

7

MAKING CONNECTIONS: INTIMACY AND COMMITMENT

OF ALL THE problems you'll face with a passive-aggressive man, the most challenging pivot around the establishment of a long-term relationship and the expression of love. His problem is with the basic components of relationships themselves: intimacy; commitment; trust; the very real threat of rejection and loss; getting close (or closer to you) and the fear it engenders.

A patient confessed to me: "Bob told me on our first date that he had just ended a five-year marriage and was too emotionally bruised to get involved in a serious relationship. He looked so vulnerable. I thought all I had to do was give him time and he'd bounce back. But it turned out that he was right. After a year, I discovered he had nothing to offer me."

Some passive-aggressive men don't seem to have the wherewithal for intimate communication—the ability to find the right language, and the maturity to express what they feel. Another woman said: "Tim won't let me know what he's going through when he's feeling bad. He changes the subject or talks so obliquely I can't figure out what's troubling him, and what I can do about it."

Using low-level hostility to create distance is another classic passive-aggressive ploy. Full-fledged battles rarely break out, but there is a constant sniping and bickering—underlying tension and smoldering resentment. A third woman told me about how her elderly father's personality had changed ever since he retired and moved into her home: "All day long he complains about trivial things, and finds fault with everything I do. Even the way I make the bed is not good enough for him. He's especially good at pointing out my failings at things he's good at. Sometimes it's as if he's competing with me." I suggested that her father's griping was a direct result of how dependent he was on her, and how unproductive he felt at this stage of his life. His irritability was an attempt to prove that he didn't need her help, when underneath he recognized just how much he did.

Intimacy is the number one issue for the passive-aggressive man to manage. His duality—his passivity and his aggression at war with each other—shows itself most vulnerable in matters of intimacy. It paralyzes him. The better you understand how intimacy, trust, giving and getting and fear of rejection affect the passive-aggressive man, the better prepared you'll be to deal with him. And you may begin to ask some hard questions: Am I seeking intimacy from a man who is incapable of that closeness? Am I seeking commitment from someone who cannot make a commitment?

A CLOSE LOOK AT MEN AND INTIMACY

What *is* this thing called intimacy? You could say it's a full expression of feelings, a way for two people who care deeply for each other to be honest. Intimacy allows both of you to be mutually dependent.

Intimacy is the truth of who you are. Intimacy has its affectionate gestures, its mutual secrets, its romance and generosity, such as doing things for the other person for the joy of it or making sacrifices when necessary. And since we're complex creatures who can't survive without language, we need clarifications, explanations and verbal affirmations. Intimacy provides them. It can't thrive on suggestion, withheld information, raised eyebrows or side glances.

Men and their problems with intimacy and commitment have been the subject of scores of books and magazine articles. The prevailing theory about why these "issues" exist goes like this:

Men who define masculinity by sexual conquest find that committing to one woman compromises their ability to continue in hot pursuit of many. Their primitive biological urges to pursue and procreate, still powerful and in operation, cannot be satisfied in one committed relationship. Is this just a case of testosterone running wild, or is it the need to prop up a fragile ego?

Both may, in fact, be true. But it is *passive-aggression* more than sex that triggers the single greatest cause of men's fears of intimacy and commitment. Whenever relationships heat up (with you, his father/mother/boss or pals), the passive-aggressive man retreats, feels put upon, unappreciated and abused. His withdrawal is an attempt to shake off what he feels is the *burden* of being a fully engaged partner. It's hard for him to satisfy your needs and wishes. Intimacy and commitment, he feels, ask too much of him.

As you might imagine, distancing himself has consequences for the passive-aggressive man, too. By making himself emotionally inaccessible, he sets up situations where it's hard for anyone to satisfy him. His behavior backfires, and it affects him as much as you.

If any behavior spoils intimacy by undermining communication, it's passive-aggression. How hard it is to live with a man who asks you to guess what he wants, and who won't own up to the right answer, when you do! How demoralizing to have to *beg* for an answer. It's also frustrating to know a man loves you and is committed to you, and to watch him systematically undo or snatch back whatever assurance he's given you.

A friend of mine and amateur chess player compared passive-aggression with the knight's move in chess. On the board, the knight can move two squares forward and one to the side. In a very real way, it describes the passive-aggressive man's intimacy games.

So it is with Kara and her boyfriend, Steve. Whenever their relationship seems to get closer (by "two moves forward"), Steve says or does something to push Kara and the relationship to the side. He almost makes it impossible for both of them to be in the same place at the same time. ("Martin says we can use his beach house at the shore, for nothing. We'll go . . . you'll love it! But you know how busy you are. And it looks like I'll be working weekends for a few months . . . so we'll see.") The side move, coming out of a big pitch (dangling a tantalizing and free vacation where they would be together) shows this man's elusiveness; keeping a promise, after all, is one kind of commitment.

What kind of relationship can you have with a man for whom closeness is threatening and commitment a kind of imprisonment? Do you need to lower your expectations to make a life with him? *Yes and no.* You need to understand how a passive-aggressive man sees life, how he measures things and from there you will have to figure out how to get your fair share. You need to define for yourself what you want from an intimate relationship, and you need to learn and accept the kind of man you're involved with.

FREE-FLOATERS AND HEAVYWEIGHTS

In my practice, I've found that passive-aggressive men can be noncommittal in two ways. The free-floater keeps you as his primary interest but will secretly date other women, all the while telling you obvious lies about where he's been and denying that there are other women in his life. The "heavyweight" can be counted on to be at your elbow all the time, but he's emotionally unavailable and immovable. He counts on you to do things for him, but *your* needs disturb him.

For some passive-aggressive men, one woman is not

enough, and for others, one is too many. Both types are equally unfulfilling.

If you meet a free-floater, he might upset your life the way Mark, a high-level government official, shook up Judy's. Mark, aristocratic-looking (belying a poverty-stricken upbringing) and handsome, but known as wily and aloof in his circle, played an expert cat-and-mouse game, not only with Judy—his girlfriend and my patient—but also with his wife.

Judy and Mark dated for two months and Judy believed she'd met the man for her. She bought his "high values"— knowing each other better before they went to bed. So though Mark always put off sex, he let Judy know he found her very desirable. Finally, they had sex. When Mark wouldn't stay the night, Judy discovered why: he was married. Several weeks later, Mark upped the ante. As Judy told me:

> I was falling in love with Mark and I was deeply hurt by his lie. After that night, I didn't see him for a few weeks, until we met, coincidentally, at a cocktail party given for a children's charity. It turned out to be co-hosted by his wife. He was smooth as silk. He introduced me to his wife. I felt he was enjoying himself immensely. I had a dreadful feeling that she knew about me, and probably other women too.

Introducing wife to lover is a kamikaze approach to passive-aggression—it's daring, hostile and self-destructive at the same time. Flaunting his unfaithfulness to both women in a setting that required decorum, free-floating Mark had "triumphed" and left Judy devastated (as, we may assume, was his wife). Judy had no way to express her anger—and for a moment thought she had no right to be angry; after all, Mark *was* married.

A similar story of perfidy was told to me by another patient, a high school French teacher. One Saturday night, Nina discovered evidence of another woman in her boyfriend Greg's medicine cabinet: a diaphragm, distinctly not hers. Nina thought she deserved an explanation—all the more so since

Greg had said he loved her. He offered a transparent lie—
that it belonged to a former girlfriend and he had forgotten
to throw it out. "Don't be so insecure," he told Nina. This
is a classic passive-aggressive turn of the tables.

Later that month, Greg finally admitted that he had been
two-timing Nina, and had "committed" to another woman.
Despite this news, Nina held on to the relationship—she
wasn't ready to break things off with Greg. Nina thought
she'd outlast Greg's "fling," then fight it out to win her man.
Greg, a classic free-floater, liked being pursued and having
the upper hand; more, he liked the game. Nina told me:

> Greg suggested that I spook Donna, "the other woman,"
> and leave my dress hanging on the outside of his closet door.
> Donna would see it the next night, and get upset. I felt *ill* when
> he said that. It was a sick game. I saw that Greg's idea of
> intimacy was to humiliate people.
>
> I still cared about him a lot and it was hard for me to imagine
> breaking off with him permanently. But I knew I had to do it
> to save my life.
>
> After I left Greg, I heard Donna had moved in with him. In
> a way, I feel sorry for her, more than I do for him.

The "heavyweight" or static passive-aggressive man plays
a whole different game of deflecting intimacy at an entirely
different pace. Richard, a thirty-three-year-old draftsman for
a large architectural firm, fits into this classic passive-aggressive mentality. Richard professes to care deeply about his
girlfriend, Katherine, with whom he is living, but he continues
to resist intimacy. Their relationship is where it was four years
ago when they first moved in together. Predictably, it has lost
its momentum.

The problem is Richard's emotional paralysis. Unable to
show his feelings or respond with affection to Katherine's
loving gestures, he's a wooden and ungiving partner. Worse,
he's stubborn, and believes his reserve is a virtue: "That's just
the way I am!" By justifying his cool, he believes he doesn't
have to make an effort to *give back* to Katherine. As non-

committal as he is, he wildly resents her if she asks him to sit down and talk about improving what they have.

One of the real sore points in their relationship, Richard told me, is his lack of attentiveness to her—not out of interest in other women, not because of workaholism, not with an obsession with working out at the gym or having to see his buddies; his ultimate withdrawal is into something that gives nothing back: television. It narcotizes him; Richard gets lost in channel switching or fantasizing about the show, depending on his mood. Each night, Richard has his routine: he changes clothes, has dinner, calls a friend back, and by 8 P.M., he's manning the set; absorbed in the screen, no matter what's on.

One evening, Richard was watching a rerun of a sitcom he'd seen several times before when Katherine asked him a question. Gruffly, Richard responded, "Don't bother me now," as if this show were a matter of grave concern to his well-being.

His response hurt and shocked Katherine. An old rerun was more important than she was. No matter what she tried to do to *connect* with him, Richard shut her out of his life. The "heavyweight" passive-aggressive man like Richard may be dependable, always there—what Katherine called, "a reliable Saturday night date"—but his is a ponderous presence, a deadweight. He's there physically, which only serves as a reminder of how emotionally absent he is. What might appear to be commitment on his part is really habit.

Later, in therapy, I asked Richard what he did when Katherine complained about his behavior. A man with a sense of humor and some insight into himself, he said, "I look up and feign attention for two minutes."

THE DELICATE MATTER OF TRUST

The simplest relationships based on trust—that of parent and child, sibling and sibling—are bound by blood ties. A child trusts that his parent will defend him, support him, feed him, protect him. A parent trusts the child will be loyal, loving, obedient. Blood ties and close friendship do not guarantee trust—Cain, Judas, Brutus—thousands of stories can be told about betrayal of brother against brother, friend against friend, parent against child. The passive-aggressive man is a tireless historian when tracing the path of betrayal in *his* history—and he knows the name and address of his every Judas. He's been damaged by whatever lapse in trust, real, exaggerated or imagined, occurred back then. More to the point, he never quite believes that others can be loyal to him now.

Since the passive-aggressive man's skewed perception is that his needs are in conflict with yours, he's afraid to let down his guard—he "knows" you will take advantage of him. He can't make himself vulnerable, because he still believes, deep down, that you will attack.

A patient recently told me a fascinating dream that hinged on a crisis in trust. It was a story, I thought, that showed hope. Don dreamed he stayed at an expensive hotel where, on his first night, he was asked to give the manager a signed blank check. When Don was ready to leave, he received a bill that he felt wasn't calculated properly, since he hadn't been given credit for his prior payment—that blank check.

How did Don interpret this? He felt he was being cheated "by his treatment" at the hotel. By probing, we discovered that Don connected me with this experience—that the "treatment" he was referring to was psychotherapy, and what the dream revealed was his fear of dependency on me. He thought that if he made himself vulnerable to me—that is, gave me a blank check—then I would take advantage of him. But Don, described by his girlfriend as mistrustful and reluctant to make himself vulnerable to her, still signed the check in his dream. He wanted the relationship.

What the dream indicated is that Don's basic mistrust is fueled by its opposite—strong dependency needs that frighten him and that he's afraid to confront. When he makes himself overly dependent on people, he feels they abuse the privilege, thus justifying his suspicions. His mixed messages make sense to him—the conundrum of "I want you, but I don't trust you," or "Can I? . . . but why would I . . . ?"

This dream is significant and revealing for a man like Don, and more important, it shows glimmerings of potential change—if still at the unconscious level—of his working out his conflict over dependency.

GIVING AND GETTING

It is generally true that when people feel gratified, they are willing and generously able to gratify others. A child raised in a home with abundant quantities of love and caring grows up knowing that love isn't a scarce resource, depleted as it's given to others. Love is a well that doesn't run dry. In contrast, the passive-aggressive man was most likely raised feeling he never got enough of what he wanted—and he *still* never gets enough of what he wants. Consequently he's less than generous with his own affections. His is a special kind of selfishness, one in which he feels righteous—depriving others of the happiness he is missing makes sense to him. He thinks, "If I don't get what I want from people, then why should I give them what they want?"

On the contrary, he may have an odd sense of entitlement when people do things for him, and he still won't give them what they want, even if all they want is appreciation.

"*He never says thank you*," women tell me. You may give the man a present, go on an errand for him, make him a special meal and he acknowledges it by explanation or anecdote, not gratitude. (Digging in, he'll say, "Lasagna? Homemade? The best I've ever tasted was in a hole-in-the-wall restaurant in Florence.") Or, you have gone on a search for a box of minicassettes for his new mini tape recorder. You can't find any after a dozen calls and an equal number of stops in stationery and record shops. You tell him, and he says, "Oh, I can always call my brother's supplier." Your efforts are *not* acknowledged. He reverts to a strange kind of self-involvement; he's either touched and can't deal with it, or pleased by your attention and worries that you expect him to reciprocate.

"He insults me when I tell him I have something for him or I want to celebrate a raise, or a birthday!" other women complain. If you tell a passive-aggressive man in advance that you have made an effort for him or feel some joy, he's suddenly anxiety-ridden about being the center of attention. Tell him you bought a small present, and he might say, "I don't need anything." Pop open a bottle of champagne, and he may feign abstinence or snort, "I hate celebrations, especially celebrations with cheap champagne." The insult knocks the wind out of your pleasure, and the mood of the evening is his now, not yours. He's safe.

"He puts me in positions that humiliate me, often over small things," other women say. It's a common complaint and a frustrating trait delivered by passive-aggressive men. It happened to Helen, a patient of mine in her early thirties, a designer of children's clothes, who's been married for five years. John, her husband, kept putting off paying a small plumber's bill until four months had passed. The plumber was phoning Helen every day now at her job, furious and threatening. Helen's husband John kept telling her—falsely—that he'd paid the man, but she knew John was holding the plumber off and would not pay until the last desperate moment.

She'd gone through it with John before—he hated paying bills, *any* bills; his quirk was to make others beg, demand or threaten legal action, including department stores, the bank, the phone company, charge cards. He was artful and persuasive on the phone—great at stalling people until they reached their limit with his excuses. Basically, John was a skillful liar.

Finally, feeling humiliated by John's lying, she decided to take the matter into her own hands; sympathetic to the plumber, Helen wrote the check. As might be expected,

John was furious, but he wouldn't discuss it. As she told the story:

> When I told John I paid the plumber, he looked at me as if I had betrayed him. I suddenly got the queasy feeling that jerking people around on the phone over money was John's way of being powerful—he enjoyed humiliating others.
>
> John was mad, but it was mostly jaw clenching and dirty looks. I'd never paid a bill with his name on it before. He told me in a strangely cold tone to mind my own business. I said the plumber was my business, too.

John has created a dynamic in which giving to others, even when they deserve it, means that he is depriving himself. Things could be otherwise, though he's not aware how.

This ingrained belief of the passive-aggressive man that he does not and will not get what he wants becomes an expectation, and the expectation itself turns into a self-fulfilling prophecy. People are not generous with someone who consistently deprives them. Since he doesn't permit himself the pleasure of enjoying life's satisfactions, he pushes people away, thereby initiating their rejection of him. Thus, his basic attitude toward life, toward himself and toward the world sets himself up for disappointment, *just as he expected*. It is a vicious cycle that creates more and more divisiveness.

If you are dealing with a man like John, whose fundamental belief is reinforced by a jaded view of his experience, then it's hard to convince him that he's sabotaging himself. He'll tell you Fate is against him, or that others have an unfair advantage over him. When he deals with you—bargaining over where to go to dinner or thrashing out an argument— this justifies his attitude of impenetrable defensiveness and unwillingness to compromise. And his sulking only makes matters worse: How can you be expected to please somebody who refuses to make his wishes known?

The passive-aggressive man sets up barriers to intimacy on both sides of the giving and getting equation.

FEELING REJECTED AND BEING REJECTED

As you've noted, relationships with a passive-aggressive man run aground, in part, because he hides his feelings, especially feelings of being rejected. The man harbors a grudge, then he takes it out on someone at a later date or in some indirect way. He feels hurt by anyone who does not accept him *exactly as he is*, and though he does not make his feelings public, you may be sure that someone will pay for it, sometime, somehow.

This case struck me as typical of the passive-aggressive man's inability to acknowledge feeling rejected. It focuses on Phil, a twenty-eight-year-old structural engineer and amateur body builder, who was helping his fiancée, Janet, type a paper she had due the next day—a paper that was critical for her master's degree in special education. When it was done, Janet felt too tense and worked up to make love with Phil. She said she'd rather talk and "hang out." Phil was disappointed and thought she was being self-centered after all he'd done for her that night. He thought she "owed" him. However, instead of telling Janet how he felt, Phil left abruptly, went home and stewed. As he saw it, there was no use in telling Janet that she'd hurt him. She had rejected him, and that was that.

In our therapy session, I asked Phil to make the distinction between feeling rejected and *being* rejected. One is subjective, and the other is objective. "I love you, but excuse me this evening," is a reasonable and sensitive way to say no. "Get out . . . you're always all over me" is a hostile and final turn-down. That Phil read rejection into situations is typical of passive-aggressive men. It seemed, in fact, that Janet was grateful for his help with the paper, and her tension was genuine. The mistake Phil made was not being willing to discuss how he felt and give Janet the opportunity to reassure him. I have no doubt that she would have; Janet wanted him and cared about him.

You must remember that a passive-aggressive man has deep feelings—and his feelings are easily hurt, even if he doesn't show it. Rebecca, another patient, told me of a recent encounter with a man she liked but wanted to get to know at a slow pace. Hank tended to be effusive; he was eager to be with her, but Rebecca told him that he was being "pushy," trying to "steamroll" her.

Hank was offended by her comments since he genuinely liked her, but he didn't say anything when she chastised him. His actions spoke for him; he didn't call back. When Rebecca finally called a week later to find out what the matter was, he said, "I didn't want to be *pushy*." Then she realized how she'd inadvertently hurt him. It surprised her; Hank appeared to be a strong and confident character. For someone who always wanted to be in control, he was remarkably fragile.

Many passive-aggressive men have great difficulty maintaining friendships and romantic relationships. Some become demoralized and assume that people won't like them *after* sustained contact. ("Once they get to know me, people will be turned off.") Because of such low self-esteem, many passive-aggressive men actively push people away. They anticipate inevitable rejection, and try to preempt it. The more they believe this, the less chance they have of forming new friendships or establishing a love relationship. Such men need to learn that they can be open to the possibility of rejection and disappointment—and *survive*.

MAKING THE FIRST CONNECTION

If the relationship is of real value to you—and if you're reading this book, it is—the most important point to keep in mind is that the passive-aggressive man is *scared*, no matter how tough his exterior. And while his behavior is not your problem and his craziness is not your fault, you play a part in this relationship, and want to do what you can to make it work.

The passive-aggressive man fears revealing himself. Showing his feelings, he believes, would leave him raw and vulnerable—you would know what bothers him, what hurts him and what about you threatens him. All his cards would be on the table. To understand his needs, you must remember that he is afraid of being dependent on you, and that he fears being attacked, humiliated or rejected for feeling this way.

Unless he feels safe, he will not make an effort to examine his behavior, never mind make a change. To change, he needs an opportunity for trust to develop—and you'll need to create that opportunity for him. Let him talk. Let him express himself, as he can. Don't psychoanalyze him or belittle him for not "confessing" enough. Don't make him feel inferior by giving him examples of how *you* would say something. Take the little indirect hints he provides about what he wants, and respond to them. Empathize with how he feels, and don't make your affection contingent on how he behaves.

The passive-aggressive man's vulnerability makes him do defiant and provocative things, but all he's trying to do is prove to others that he doesn't need them. But he does. And intensely.

When we talk about "communication" between men and women, we're describing more than just framing a sentence to impart some sort of information; there are also the nuances of language, attitude (or body language), tone, approach, timing, a sense of romance, chemistry, the ability to build a sense of intimacy and, *most important*, respect and regard for another's opinions and feelings.

What we value about communication is more than someone's being an articulate, authentic companion. Real communication touches a nerve; you are tuned in to each other, listen between the lines and empathize. You feel *connected* to the other person, with give and take. Love, and its expression, is difficult for the passive-aggressive man. It's up to you to keep the connection alive.

Ideally, relationships are based on deep affection and respect, and most important, *acceptance* of who the other is. Very few couples sustain love relationships over time without demands, expectations and inevitable disappointments. We're all flawed, imperfect, which is all right. What matters is acknowledging what you need and who you are, to understand what you want from a relationship—and what, realistically, the passive-aggressive man you're with can give.

Love shouldn't be confused with passion or compelling sexuality, with submission or domination. Love shouldn't be confused with a campaign to tell others how you intend to "fix" their lives. You have no responsibility to make a passive-aggressive man happy, and it is misdirected energy to set out as the instrument of change for someone you love. Resolving your problems with a passive-aggressive man and changing the relationship is a real possibility, but the measure of success, as in any partnership, takes the two of you wanting to make it work.

In the next chapter I'll take a much closer look at intimate relationships, and discuss how to have a satisfying sexual relationship with a passive-aggressive man.

8

SEX AND THE PASSIVE-AGGRESSIVE MAN

A MALE MOVIE star, the story goes, plays an interesting game of seduction with women. The moves—and the rules—remain his, which he plays out until he wins what he wants: surrender. It's a simple game: the Star comes on strong, offers a night of great sex, but makes no promises about the future. The women who accept his invitation go willingly, excited by his good looks, celebrity and power. They eagerly anticipate going to bed with him, even hoping they'll touch him as no other woman has and move into his life.

As the Star knowingly toys with each woman, she falls for him. The more he turns her on, the more she's hot for him—the kind of response that warms him. When it's hot enough, his moment of truth boils to the surface: the Star cuts the rendezvous short with a telling remark, "You want me now . . . but where were you before I was famous?" In a final move, he refuses to have sex. Women leave feeling disappointed, foolish and confused. And of course, there *is* no answer for someone who wants you to make a difference in his past and humiliates you because you cannot.

The passive-aggressive man has struck again, deftly and unexpectedly, undermining one of your most vulnerable points: your sexuality.

What does the Star get out of this? He plays a game that satisfies him for the moment. He wants you to want him, but he doesn't want to want you in return. He makes you suffer for the wanting, too, leading you on instead of just graciously ending the evening with no one feeling rejected. The Star's pattern is so established that he operates on automatic pilot.

The identity of the Star doesn't matter. The point is that passive-aggressive behavior, this time personified as "the tease," finds its place in the bedroom too. The Star in question may be different from the man in your life because he has celebrity status, but his power and money haven't fundamentally changed him. It affects his ability to commit to a relationship, it reinforces his fear of intimacy—and it makes for an often unsatisfying sex life.

THE PASSIVE-AGGRESSIVE LOVER

Sex is a complex interaction for all of us, all the more so for the passive-aggressive man sharing your bed. Sex triggers his fears of intimacy, dependency and competition, all of which set up barriers to mutual sexual satisfaction.

The external details of sex may torment him if he's especially insecure. He'll agonize over how he "measures up" to other men—his physical appeal or penis size or his sexual performance. Acutely aware of what he imagines women want from him sexually, he feels pressured and he doesn't function well under the strain. By turning an act of pleasure and intimacy into little more than hormones, chemistry and imminent conquest, he corrupts the experience for himself and for you.

Sex should be freeing, but open physical contact scares him. He worries: Will he reveal too much of himself when he's excited by passion and physical abandonment? He hopes not. Since the passive-aggressive man *can* be emotionally moved, he dreads the moment when his feelings put him "at the mercy of a woman." He wants to appear strong, in control of his body—and yours. But the prospect of giving up control terrifies him.

The sexual impulse, a basic human drive, is closely linked to aggression. There is a primitive, sensually abandoned quality to sex that, while it arouses pleasure, may also encourage the direct expression of hostility. It's the kind of animalistic release that moves some men to playful biting and others to greater degrees of brutality. Sex can also arouse an *indirect* expression of hostility in some men. Since passive-aggression is a version of aggression, anything fueling one is likely to ignite the other.

If you have dated, loved or lived with a passive-aggressive man, then you know the ways this man is a virtuoso of sexual elusiveness. The sexual arena, after all, provides an ideal opportunity for him to invent games and make you his primary opponent. The most potent of these games have to do with attitudes about and leading up to sex. As he sees it, a bedroom may well become a battleground, and a sexual encounter, a life or death challenge.

Psychological conflicts about sex are intensified for a passive-aggressive man with doubts about himself as an effective, functioning, potent male. Let's take a closer look at the kind of sex games the passive-aggressive man plays and may be playing with you.

SEXUAL PREFERENCES

THE TEASE: A WAY OF DEALING WITH INSECURITY

The tease draws you in with his gift of charm or boyish appeal, but like the Star he doesn't come through. If you feel you've been led on, you have. He persists in tantalizing you, withholding sex with every come-on, unless and until he decides he wants you after all. But what goes around comes around, and it's not just you who is affected, or even hurt, by sexual passive-aggression. Take the following case.

Paul, a twenty-seven-year old partner in a money-management firm, recently entered therapy because of serious doubts about his ability to succeed, both in a career and with women. He was so self-conscious about every move he made, it sabotaged him, most often, sexually. He told me a revealing story about trying to connect with a woman, and if you've known a tease, Paul's version will probably strike a familiar chord.

One night he met a woman at a party and flirted enough with her to pique her interest. When he suggested they leave and go for a drink, Joan happily agreed to it—she was clearly attracted to him. She found him funny and appealing, and the chemistry seemed to bubble. After two drinks, Paul suggested they leave. He said:

> Joan got that look of expectancy. When I saw it, I felt a sense of dread. Don't ask me why. I could have stayed the night with her, easily, but I freaked. I said goodbye and jumped in a taxi, leaving Joan standing there on the street, rejected, and certainly confused.

What happened here? Paul is the passive-aggressive man at his most "teasing"—giving you less than he implies he has, less than you want, but enough to lead you on for more. Once he has you hooked, he cuts you off—suddenly and cleanly. Even if he sees that you're not interested at first, he works at charming you, tantalizing you and creating a need in you . . . and then turns you down. It is brinksmanship par excellence.

The passive-aggressive tease is not unaware of what he's doing. Some men fight the truth and play innocent ("I decided I didn't want her that much after all. Going through the motions wasn't worth it"), while others struggle with the problem. Paul had glimmers of what was going on below the surface: he was afraid of rejection. Since most women brought out these fears, he wouldn't make a *real* sexual advance, waiting for them to make the first move. Paradoxically, this made him feel more in control. Since sex (or no sex) was up to Joan, why make himself vulnerable? By doing nothing other than just *being* there, he became the object of desire, and sought after. It boosted his self-esteem. But even then, once Joan made the first move, Paul still wasn't ready to show his vulnerability, and he ran away.

Over time, Paul learned to face his insecurity, tune in to how he treated women and acknowledge that his games really gave him very little in return. Eventually, he was able to show his vulnerable side to women, trust them or accept rejection without overinvesting in passive-aggression as a defense— and a way of life.

THE PASSIVE PARTNER: DEALING WITH SUBMISSION AND DOMINATION

Not only are some passive-aggressive men able to separate sex and intimacy, but many like to be sexually overpowered and prefer the company of "dominating women." This is the kind of control they fight against out of bed, but *in* bed, the idea of surrender to a woman is exciting.

"I lie back and do nothing while she's on top. I let her do all the work," some men explain, enjoying the passivity of the position. The sexual position is not in and of itself unusual, but a single component makes it different for the passive-aggressive man: the pressure to "perform" is off. He just needs to contribute his body, passively, unmoving, if not selfishly, to create an ideally pleasurable experience for himself.

Arthur, a fairly dynamic lawyer with a growing practice specializing in criminal law, wages fearsome courtroom battles against male or female colleagues, but sexual gratification for him requires "sexually aggressive" women—a telling misuse of the term, since what he means is sexually *assertive*. He likes women to initiate sexual contact and take responsibility for their own pleasure. Feeling overburdened by a woman's sexual demands that he'd just as soon ignore, he is relieved when women gratify themselves. He's with a partner, but each of them is really having a solitary sexual experience.

Arthur explained his view to me:

Women are not as they appear on first impression. They say they want a liberated man, but they don't. What they really want is to lie back and enjoy it. They're not as liberated as they claim to be. Well, I want to lie back and enjoy it too, but they don't like it if I do.

A passive-aggressive man, seeking out *his idea* of a powerful woman, is bound to transform any interaction with her into one of woman above/man below. Women cease to be sexual partners—they're competitors instead. What Arthur is saying is, "Who will be satisfied here . . . me or her?" By implication, he's setting up a sexual track meet, a race for who wins pleasure and who loses it. The idea that mutual satisfaction is possible escapes him.

It's Arthur's passive side that compels him to set up relationships in which he feels subjectively weaker. However much a passive-aggressive man complains that women seek to control him, whether in a sexual or nonsexual context, a very basic part of him thrives on his "being taken care of," pampered, just like early childhood, when he didn't have to do much but *be there* for his mother.

Since the pleasure of *passivity* during sex lets him return to a childlike state, the image/memory of an assertive woman reassures him that someone is still around to protect him. But he's ambivalent about his passivity. While he enjoys it, he bridles at being in a weak and dependent position—even if he put himself there voluntarily. Unfortunately, if you're the woman who is unwittingly used as a pawn in his internal psychosexual drama, you may not be appreciated for what you have given him. What makes him so withholding is that he won't give what he's sure he won't get.

The paradox of Arthur's behavior is that he's not as self-serving and narcissistic as he seems. His unwillingness to satisfy a woman generously in return reflects his inability confidently to assume the mantle of manhood. It's something he's still psychologically unprepared to do. We're dealing with a thirty-five-year-old-man with a deep-seated inhibition.

To be a man means that Arthur must make his own choices, move toward independence, stand up for himself, struggle toward what he wants *without* his parents protecting him. He must fight his battles, make his decisions and set up his own standards. Growing up also means competing with other men—in Oedipal terms, "winning" his mother and vanquishing his father, his first competitor. This prospect scares Arthur two ways—he's afraid of retaliation *and* he's afraid that if he wins, he'll be in charge and will have to lead. And so he chooses otherwise: to withdraw from direct sexual competition. As he does not satisfy a woman sexually, he feels, subconsciously, that he poses less of a threat to other men.

THE WOMANIZER: HIS VERSION OF WANTING IT ALL

While passionate love brings with it affirmation of one's lovableness and the joy of giving oneself to another, the womanizing passive-aggressive man is obsessed with newness, not love. For him, each conquest holds out renewed hope for building up his sense of self—the affirmation that he's a man that women desire. And so it's conquest he's after.

An indifferent "lover" like Arthur is grudgingly sexual, but the promiscuous passive-aggressive man is mindlessly so. What they have in common is a knack for avoiding intimacy by keeping women at arm's length. The Womanizer is interested only in arousal—his relationships are primarily physical and demeaning to his partner. Any woman who says yes to him is devalued; she is there for the sport and nothing else. Commitment is not a word that comes easily to his mind and brings a smile to his lips. *If* he's able to go beyond sex and actually make an effort to have a relationship, it will be a struggle for him to stay involved. He may be a sexier guy, but he's as unavailable and disappointing as the submissive lover. Before you know it, he's on the lookout for a new woman, and a renewal of his sense of self.

Norman, a thirty-nine-year-old broker, established a pattern of serial sexual encounters with women in their early twenties, preferably recent immigrants who were sexually innocent. Most of these women were brought up in cultures that insulated women from worldly experiences. Once in the States, they looked for American men to marry, not as sexual entertainment.

Their ingenuousness appealed to Norman, who took great pride in "liberating" them from their Old World restraints. He enjoyed artfully getting them to bed and deflowering them and the sexual power he soon exercised over them. He prided himself on being a great lover and much in demand. The rub was: once they were sexually experienced, he lost interest in them.

Why did Norman set up this imaginary drama where he played "the swashbuckler," and inexperienced women, the victims? The answer is obvious: a true balance of power would make Norman feel insecure. Like Arthur, he's caught in a fear of dependency, but unlike him, he fights it by vanquishing women who cannot possibly make him feel weak by comparison.

PROBLEMS AND DEMANDS

All bedtime stories taken from the life of the passive-aggressive man eventually come around to his unwillingness to satisfy a woman—if not spiritually, then physically. He can be coolly selfish during sex, concerned primarily with his own satisfaction and oblivious to, or unconcerned about, a woman's needs. While most men will find out what it is their partner most enjoys, the passive-aggressive man may at first make an effort to please her, and later on "forgets" or complies so grudgingly that it's no longer enjoyable for her.

Whether he is being contrary, hostile or frightened, sexual problems between you two will erupt in a number of ways. Chief among them is:

WHEN HE TURNS AWAY: THE MEANING BEHIND ABSTINENCE

Resentment, exhaustion, boredom, stresses—every couple experiences setbacks and dry periods. If such problems persist, they inevitably dampen passion or bring it to a halt. The resentful passive-aggressive man is no exception. In fact, he often uses outright sexual refusal as his main weapon as he does battle with you.

Abstinence is a common complaint from women involved with passive-aggressive men. If he's in a financial pinch, he'll take you out for the evening but remind you that the evening's expenses are a huge burden. He'll then make you pay by refusing to have sex. But if you offer to go Dutch before he suggests it, he'll take it as an emasculating gesture. And still he'll make you pay by withholding sex. His sexual refusal, however, will usually be hidden under the guise of a transparent excuse: he's sleepy, sick, preoccupied with work.

Although a passive-aggressive man may never acknowledge it, aggression underlies his sexually withholding behavior. Distracted by the smokescreen of his excuses and twisted justifications, you can easily doubt yourself. You wonder if you're sufficiently attractive or sexually exciting to him, too demanding or not open enough to play with his fantasies. You think that maybe *you're* the one with a lowered sex drive. Maybe you're the cause of his "headache." As you go down this self-deprecating line of thought, and assume the blame, the passive-aggressive man's guerrilla tactics are proven successful once again.

Abstinence comes easily to a man for whom sex is not about giving and intimacy so much as proving something to himself. If he inflicts frustration on you by being withholding, he's well aware of it. His need to withhold has a history: it's a replay of the frustration and deprivation he experienced during childhood. In anticipation of being deprived or victimized again, he strikes first, depriving or victimizing you. If, covering his tracks by blaming sleepiness, stress from work, a bad dinner, he upsets you, he's triumphed doubly. To undermine your self-worth without taking action himself is a passive-aggressive man's ideal crime of omission.

IMPOTENCE

Not all passive-aggressive men are prone to sexual dysfunction, and not all sexual dysfunction is due to passive-aggression. The two sexual dysfunctions most often related to passive-aggressive personality conflicts are an inability to get and maintain an erection and premature ejaculation.

Both of these sexual problems relate to a passive-aggressive man's failure to satisfy his partner. In each case, he claims he wants to satisfy a woman, but something interferes with accomplishing his goal. He's oddly disconnected from his problem, too. He believes that any sexual problem, such as impotence, is outside his control, unrelated to his mental attitudes. A passive-aggressive man, at his worst, can wallow in the crisis of sexual failure ("Okay, so I'm *slow* about sex. I guess it's low drive, so what can I do?"), but deny any responsibility for it.

Potency and impotence are among the most sensitive issues for men, especially for an insecure passive-aggressive man. And if he has problems with his masculinity, the inability to get and maintain an erection is sure to be a source of great embarrassment. But he'll defend himself in passive-aggressive style.

Impotence almost always reveals anxiety and anger—and it's a difficult subject for men to talk about. Ronald, a thirty-eight-year-old business consultant, recently divorced, consulted with me because of occasional impotence. He was "ashamed" of his problem, saying it made him feel "weak . . . a wimp."

As I questioned him, I found Ron viewed women as both dangerous yet fragile. Women confused him; he thought they could be emotional blackmailers with unpredictable hair-trigger tempers. Most of all, Ron thought that the women in his life lashed out at him at the slightest threat to their self-esteem.

The clues to his perception of women as incendiary creatures are found in his early life. Ron's mother had not allowed him to express his natural aggressive instincts—she told him anger would make him "crazy" and hurt everyone around him. He feared being "put away." His mother came across as a genteel woman trying to keep the peace, but was actually competitive with Ron and his father, who traveled a lot. She resented the fact that Ron was male, or I should say, that she was *not*. Using his mother as a model for women in general, Ron squelched the aggressive side of his maleness, suffering further because he had no outlet for his anger. The fact that his father was on the road so much didn't help, either.

The connection between an overbearing mother and his occasional impotence began to make sense to Ron. Functioning as a man, having and sustaining an erection, meant being an aggressive male, a role he was afraid to assume.

There was a second breakthrough. In a later session, Ron told me about a dream in which he unintentionally shot and killed his girlfriend. He interpreted this dream as reflecting a second and related meaning to his impotence: he made his penis a gun, a weapon that could destroy the women he had sex with. His impotence expressed his guilt about hating and fearing women and wanting to hurt them—and it also restrained him from "going crazy" and killing someone (with his penis).

It was finally clear what Ron meant during our very first session when he said he was both embarrassed and "gunshy" about going to bed with women. We now understood the real meaning of those words.

PREMATURE EJACULATION

Premature ejaculation may not always be caused by psychological factors, but when it *is* a symptom of unresolved problems, it's a sexual path the passive-aggressive man may take. Quick to orgasm, he can still create a sense of participating in sex without, and before, satisfying a woman. His apparent interest and activity may, in fact, cover an underlying passivity and selfishness.

In another guise, premature ejaculation is a form of teasing. It's all the more disheartening for the woman aroused by a man who can't satisfy her.

GETTING TOGETHER: STEPS FOR MAKING THE SEXUAL RELATIONSHIP WORK

Sexual incompatibility is almost always a sign of problems in the relationship in general—problems with communication; difficulty dealing with anger, dependency and intimacy; performance anxiety. In the rare instances where sexual dysfunction is not itself indicative of broader relationship issues, it is bound to spill over into other spheres and cause conflicts in the relationship. What this means is that sexuality can never be considered separately from the total relationship. Improving one will improve the other.

Jim's story is a good example. Although they had formerly been ardent, Jim and his wife hadn't had sex in over a year, nor would he talk with Alma about what was bothering him. When I first saw him, he believed he had lost the desire for sex in general, which was not tied to his feelings for Alma specifically. Alma, on the other hand, had long before sought to save her dignity by avoiding further rejection, and had surrendered her campaign to seduce Jim back.

What got Jim and Alma into this knotty misunderstanding? Silly as it may seem, Alma had once, about a year earlier, turned Jim down when she just didn't want to have sex, and he'd been angry about it ever since. Jim can't appreciate Alma's point of view, nor, more critically, is he able to see *how things have changed*. Jim is a grudge collector, and doggedly holds on to this past slight: Alma refused him one time, and now *he* will reject *her* all the time.

Jim is a man haunted by a single rejection. How do you handle passive-aggressiveness in such a frustrating situation?

There are some fundamental personality issues at work here. At the deepest level, Jim is angry at women. He constantly tries to find reasons why, and occasions when, women let him down. And so he holds on to little disturbances and minor rejections. The poet Carl Sandburg said "the past is a bucket of ashes," but for some passive-aggressive men, the past is a bucket of glowing embers, if not in flames, then hot enough. So while you can do little about past history, you can do something about restructuring a more hopeful future together.

Your problem may not be exactly like Jim and Alma's, but in most cases, the same dynamics drive all passive-aggressive men. Connecting with him emotionally and sexually is not an impossible task. Once you understand where his inhibition and ambivalence come from—*fear of dependency, fear of intimacy, submerged anger, and performance anxiety*—you can help defuse their power over him.

These fears are going to emerge as a sexual relationship with a passive-aggressive man evolves. And should you reach a sexual stalemate, then it's up to you to call attention to the problem. Improved communication is necessary for rekindling passion—it opens up channels for expressing love and affection, and helps him to get in touch with his feelings. Reassurance works by assuaging the passive-aggressive man's performance anxiety.

These are vulnerable issues for the passive-aggressive man, as they are for you, so you will have to be diplomatic—know what to bring up and what to keep silent about. Don't come at him with both barrels. The key thing for you to remember during these conversations is that men like Jim are suffused by fear, no matter how strong they appear.

Using Jim's case, let's go through the two main barriers to sexual satisfaction.

COMMUNICATION

A passive-aggressive man has difficulty connecting sex with intimacy, and one way it comes out is by noncommunication.

When Alma turned Jim down, Jim's feelings were hurt beyond what the situation called for. Alma doesn't know that she's been repeatedly rejected because of that turndown. And even if she did, she would not know why the "punishment" (prolonged abstinence and rejection) does not fit "the crime." This is a problem with communication in general, not merely with sexual disinterest.

Jim's feelings are running the situation, so Alma needs to be the one to improve communication. She should appeal to his reason, speak firmly but caringly and try not to use an accusatory tone of voice.

With a man like Jim, it's important to present the facts first: a problem exists, and the two of you have to do something about it before it ruins the relationship. Ask him if he values the relationship, and is willing to make changes to keep it going.

Then, point out to him what you think he's doing—for example, obsessing over the past and blowing out of proportion the meaning of a common occurrence between couples. Ask him what he gains by holding on to an old slight. Neither one of you gains anything.

Finally, show him how it benefits him to let go of old slights that have no bearing on what's happening now. Reassure him that he is important to you, and tell him that you hope you are just as important to him. Help him to feel less threatened and less embattled. He must feel safe before he can open up.

A lack of communication hurts sexual pleasure as much after the act as before. Many women tell me that they either feel used ("I went to bed with him, and now he acts like he doesn't know my name. . . ." or "He seems to like me, except when we're in bed. He won't talk to me. . . .") or full of self-doubt. ("What have I done wrong?") Being angry or blaming yourself misses the point with this man. By being angry at him, you'll only make things worse. He can't open up to his feelings when he is being accused of abusing yours. And blaming yourself is clearly not a good way to improve communication.

Women ask me, sometimes in mystified tones: "What does

he think will happen if he appears vulnerable?" "How could he not trust me?" "Why does he think I'd humiliate him? I care for him and love him."

The passive-aggressive man is a champion at denying his feelings, especially when they have been aroused during sex. Denial can run strong for him—he'll deny how powerful the experience was, how important you are or how exciting it was for him. Afraid of the power his feelings have over him, he hopes to defuse and diminish them, to find some way of controlling them. To allow you to see how much he cares about you is terrifying to him, so he withdraws in response. This is when he grows quiet, turns away, immediately drops off to sleep, or, if you're not living together, gets dressed and leaves in the middle of the night.

The passive-aggressive man believes that if he gets emotionally attached to a woman during sex, he will be all the more dependent on her. Jim, for example, wants to feel he doesn't need Alma even though she's his wife. He rejects sex and denies his feelings. He has gone the limit. Other passive-aggressive men can perform and have sex, and then reject intimacy, splitting it off from sexuality.

What can you do?

If you feel shut out, don't confront a passive-aggressive man head-on with, "I know you care about me. Why can't you just let your emotions *out*?" This merely reminds him of his fears—among them that you are setting yourself up as his superior.

Help him show his feelings gradually, not through harshly dealt interactions where defending himself against your judgments takes priority. Keep talking to him, no matter how innocuous the conversation, rather than fall into silence. Move out of issues such as "the state of our relationship" or "I love you, do you love me?" to more neutral ground. Getting an easy communication back and forth helps bring the passive-aggressive man out of his shell. But you have to know when to stop.

Since these men talk about anything *but* how they feel, you

need to give them the space they need to roam about emotionally. Eventually, you can bring the subject around to feelings, but don't storm the barricades, telling him how distant
he is or that he has no heart, to keep you dangling on so
tenuous a string. Behave in ways that are more lovingly accepting of him; tell him you love him, if you want to, but in
a way that doesn't make him believe he's required to respond
in kind or that he has to protect his privacy. Tell him how
you feel at times when he's most relaxed, not when feelings
are likely to come up and scare him, such as during and after
sex. Discussions of love often are most clarifying during the
calmest of times.

PERFORMANCE ANXIETY

The question eventually arises from women involved with
passive-aggressive men: If the guy's lost interest in sex, is it
something she's done? Is it her appearance—that is, does she
no longer turn him on? More often than not, it's not your
problem, and you shouldn't devalue your sense of self. So if
we can successfully put to one side the self-esteem issue as it
affects you, we can look at what's bothering him about the
act of sex: performance anxiety.

Performance, for a man, means tapping into his sexuality
and sexual desire, getting and maintaining an erection, satisfying a woman and satisfying himself. Some men may have
no problem with potency, but have little instinct as lovers
when it comes to pleasing a woman. The guy may not have
"technique" or passion, or know what to do to excite or
please a woman—and with it, the inability to ask her what
she likes and how she likes it.

Jim's performance anxiety typifies many passive-aggressive
men and the hot-button issues that disturb them: he fears
he's lost his desire for sex, he's anxious about pleasing Alma
and he worries about *showing* her how much he loves her.
He wishes she didn't matter so much to him, but since she
does, he pushes her away psychologically by making her the

"enemy"—the woman who may turn on him and humiliate him. The passive-aggressive man in your life probably shares these feelings.

Before you can show the passive-aggressive man that he *does* still have an interest in sex, you need to be clear about what bothers him. Get it out in the open and over with. Label his fear, whether it's anger, fear of showing deeper feelings, worry about being a good lover.

Many men (passive-aggressive or not) cannot talk with women about their fears regarding sex. As a psychotherapist, I can more easily ask the guy, What is it that you're afraid of? That she won't have an orgasm? That she won't like your style? What will happen afterward? Interestingly, when I bring up the issues so concretely, it's much less threatening to him than he thinks it will be. Like many night fears, once you turn the light on them, they go away.

However, such a talk is probably out of line for you: with a passive-aggressive man, such confessional openness might humiliate him. The specter of humiliation casts a long shadow in this man's psyche. If he tries his best at sex and fails in any way, that, for him, is humiliation. His manhood has been tested, found wanting and his partner knows it. So if he doesn't try, he will never fail. If perpetual anger at you will keep him from failing, then he'll choose anger over pleasure. Just like Jim.

What a passive-aggressive man has lost touch with in the morass of what he thinks others expect of him is his own desire. He has forgotten what he wants sexually and how it feels. The more you can help him rediscover how much he wants sex, the more willingly he'll partake.

If he feels that you're demanding too much from him and he can't satisfy you, he may be reluctant to confide in you or he will tell you indirectly. So tell him what pleases you and that he gratifies you when you do make love. This will build his confidence. Your strategy is to get out of a combat zone and improve communication. Sex is not an arena where you can set limits and deliver ultimatums—everything has to be done willingly and be freely given.

By depriving women of sexual pleasure, and with it, honest affection and caring, a passive-aggressive man also deprives himself of a meaningful connection to another. As George Vaillant writes in *Adaptation to Life*, "passive-aggressive behavior is surprisingly provocative; for in turning anger against the self, one by no means spares other people." We see this clearly in the bedroom.

These ideas can help you begin changing and rebuilding an intimate, sexual relationship with a passive-aggressive man. Change is an astonishing thing; as you continue to turn around this relationship, you'll change too. The benefits of change may even affect you first: the more deliberate your actions, the more conscious you are of motivations and the emotional and sexual landscape surrounding the passive-aggressive man, the more you'll appreciate your value as a healthy human being.

9

MARRIAGE AND PARENTHOOD

WHILE MARRIAGE OFFERS a domain for the most intimate and supportive of relationships, for a passive-aggressive man, it also represents the front line of battle. He can come to grips with his behavior or, stuck in the past, continue to play out his problems with intimacy and communication in the bosom of matrimony. He can take out his anger and insecurity on the very people he loves the most or finally be willing to give up his game playing, indirectness and emotional withdrawal for their well-being.

Making a long-term commitment and forging a meaningful partnership can offer him a sense of comfort he missed when he was single. With marriage, he's no longer living for himself. *He's got more to lose* if he doesn't make an effort to show compassion for your feelings, regard for your opinions and respect for you.

Every marriage has a honeymoon period where euphoria bathes everything in a soft pink light. Under such a rosy glow, even the passive-aggressive man at his noncommunicative worst may appear like the romantic, strong, silent type. Sometimes words *aren't* necessary between partners who connect with each other intensely and fully. But when real life unavoidably intervenes, you'll find his silence isn't heroic, and your misunderstandings become impossible to ignore; his broken promises, his insistence on solitude and his need for control become relentless. Before you know it, *you're living with passive-aggressive behavior every day.*

There's an unspoken rule in many marriages: you have to know when to overlook certain of your spouse's neurotic tics (he won't step on a wet bathmat; he tells you in an authoritative manner what you already know or may have even told *him* the day before) and say nothing, to keep the peace. This works both ways. Perfection is not part of the human condition; you're not perfect and neither is he.

The truth is, there will always be conflicts between couples who care about each other. Conflict *isn't* a failing but an opportunity to speak your mind, tell the other person what bothers or hurts you and what you want. As a psychotherapist, I counsel many married couples who are unable to discuss their problems. Marriage to a passive-aggressive man can make such problems harder to figure out, since his modus operandi is to becloud and confuse, imply and deflect.

Your marriage has a good chance of working, once you identify certain key behaviors the passive-aggressive husband (and father) uses.

First, let's start with a caveat to *you.*

ADOPTING HIS STYLE

Living with a passive-aggressive man can have a residual drawback: you may begin to adopt his approach, more as a tactic (to keep the peace) than a defense (to beat him at his own game). His style—such as the subtlety of his indirectness—insinuates itself into the relationship. Both of you soon fall into speaking around issues and relating through misunderstandings.

Plotlines in sitcoms and soap operas often operate around the premise of misunderstanding, but they're resolved through gags, car chases and excessive explanatory dialogue within the half hour or hour. In real life, misunderstandings aren't as amusing and few of them are resolved in record time. The point is *not to be swept along by recurrent misunderstandings and miscommunications*, not to be pacified by passive-aggressive logic and begin using it yourself. With honest communication, there is no mystery. Passive-aggression puts both of you in a state of denial, *unclear* about the subject of your fight or discussion.

Take Anna and Don. Anna, a thirty-year-old manager of a boutique, has been married to Don for eight years. Hoping to have a romantic time alone with Don, she suggested in a playful and affectionate way that they take a second honeymoon. Don's response was ambiguous if not confusing. He told her:

> That's an idea. I have to figure out how much it'll cost and see if we can really spare the money for the trip. How long did you want to go for? And, anyway, if we go, the kids should come along, don't you think?

This double (and overexplained) message bothered Anna: Did Don want to go or not? Had he missed the point that the trip was about rekindling romance, not about a family vacation or how much it would cost? Or did he get the point and just wanted to avoid being alone with her? Discouraged by his covert insult, Anna dropped the subject.

Anna had become so used to Don's indirectness that over the course of their eight years together, she'd taken on some of his characteristics. Most notably, she'd begun to avoid conflict and no longer picked up on his responses. She'd given up. By this point, she rarely insisted on further clarification. Instead, she became as oblique as Don, missing out on the intimacy she sought and needed.

How did it happen? Patterns like this one appear at the beginnings of a marriage and grow insidiously. Early on, Anna saw that when she spoke openly and sincerely to Don, he didn't respond. This left her feeling vulnerable and isolated, and eventually, she felt safer hiding her feelings—just like Don. This is a very real way for passive-aggression to lead to an erosion of trust in marriage. It must be avoided.

Be aware of how *you* respond when you get an answer, or a nonanswer, from your husband. If you find yourself giving in too easily just to get along with him, face up to your frustrations. Unless you plead your case and stand your ground your best interests will be lost in the shuffle. He won't do it for you. Avoiding conflict may bring you temporary comfort, but ultimately, you'll have to decide what you're really getting out of playing his game.

SUPPORT AND CRITICISM: HIS MISPERCEPTIONS OF MOTIVES

The passive-aggressive man is notorious for trying the patience of even the most forgiving wife. At some point, she's bound to reach her limit—especially if he's disappointed her one time too many. She's bound to criticize him, and when she does, she'll be perceived, to a greater or lesser extent, as the controlling mother. The Rescuer (a woman he counts on) turns into the Jailer (a woman he fears). This provides a passive-aggressive husband with all the justification he needs to feel persecuted.

Even when he acknowledges the efforts she makes on his behalf, he may minimize her comments and lash out, calling her names, "bitch . . . nitpicker . . ." and demanding that she "get off my back." Somehow or other, wives who call attention to his shortcomings are to blame—for everything and for nothing! Criticize a passive-aggressive husband, and he'll believe that you don't understand him. In return, you run the risk of provoking his temper or a bout of petulant sulking.

Pam's case illustrates how a passive-aggressive husband can mistake criticism (even when it's friendly and helpful) for domination.

Pam's husband, Ken, was being interviewed for an important job in a Fortune 500 company, where he might be offered a major executive position and a substantial salary increase. Excited about the prospect of Ken's moving up in his profession, Pam innocently suggested that he buy a new suit for the interview. This irritated Ken, who told her, "Mind your own business." Why the hostile response, especially from a man like Ken who revels in being taken care of?

It's the inevitable twist of passive-aggressive logic.

Ken heard in Pam's suggestion *solely* an ulterior motive for wanting him to get the promotion—it would mean a salary raise for him and *more money for her to spend*. He missed her true intent: enthusiastic support of his efforts and pride in his accomplishment. Ken's misinterpretation of her financial expectations put additional pressure on him to perform well. It gave him someone to thwart. Pam was transformed in his mind into a dominating, even persecutory, figure, and he retaliated by sabotaging the interview and being turned down for the job. He converted his failure into her failure as well, so that both Pam and Ken ended up feeling like victims.

There's another side to Ken. On occasion, he explodes at Pam for expecting too much of him and then acts contrite, asking for her forbearance. To make sure he gets her sympathy, he makes self-deprecatory remarks, which he hopes she will counter. ("Oh, Ken, you're too hard on yourself. You're so hard-working and smart. . . .") The more sympathy Pam shows him, the more she restrains herself from making further demands. Finally, Ken's round of temper/apology/plea for comfort manipulates Pam into a placating, rather than critical, position. It's easier for both of them to take, but neither one gets what they want.

Self-doubt, fear of achievement and fear of failing are mortared into the wall the passive-aggressive man has built around himself. He devalues himself, often giving money the place of honor on the parapets. Therefore, when Pam, for example, approaches him, Ken thinks she's on a crusade for the treasure—not his soul, but his cash.

Making money, others' expectations that he must be a success and a fear of achievement are big problems in the life of this man. If your spouse, like Ken, believes your motive is money—that you're asking him how he did because you care only about his future earnings—he's probably confused. Be clear that *you're on his side.* It will help to say to him, "If I've been too pushy about the money, I'll back off. I'm not spending it before you earn it. When it comes, we can figure out what to do with it." If he is setting up a situation where he ruins his chances of promotion *just to deprive you of what he thinks you want,* it's only self-defeating.

I suggested in the previous chapter that there will be occasions when you need to remind the passive-aggressive man of how much he wants sex; the same principle can be applied here: remind him that *he* wants to achieve for himself, not just for you. Remind him that he's interested in the promotion and what it will garner—more prestige, access to more of the things he wants. Emphasize the accomplishment and self-esteem, not the cash.

MY WAY . . . OR NO WAY AT ALL

Many wives complain that their passive-aggressive husbands live in a world of black-and-white, where options are limited and freedom of choice is restricted. These wives describe a man who doesn't believe in compromise, other people's interests or in treading the wide and amicable territory called "the middle ground." By limiting options in so forceful a manner, the passive-aggressive man controls events and you.

He may be indirect and ambiguous, but this man still wants to take charge of marital decisions. As his wife, you may not know what he wants, but he nonetheless expects you to abide by his choices, which may or may not reflect what *he* really wants. Andrew is a good example of this convoluted type of authority.

Feeling benevolent, Andrew would ask his wife, Sandy, to choose a restaurant. He'd go along with her, but express his dissatisfaction by grimacing when the menu arrived; getting angry at the waiter; demanding a dish they did not make;

disparaging his dinner, no matter how good or bad it was, describing it as "expensive crap," or even "forgetting" his wallet.

Andrew was good at ruining everyone's evening because "his discerning taste" had been violated by someone else's choice. If Sandy told him that he was being selfish and rude, Andrew would pout and play the victim. He was "made to" eat food he didn't like in a restaurant he had had no say in choosing. It made no difference to point out that he'd given the choice to Sandy. When the passive-aggressive wants things his way or no way at all, he will always be able to come up with an answer.

Handling the autocrat is a challenge. This guy has lost his way on the road to compromise. In real life, some situations are straightforward: flap A must be inserted in slot B for object C to work. In most other cases, there is a wide swing of how something can be done, said or felt—how you dress, the friends you choose, whether you organize paperwork "by piles or files," whether or not you are willing to pay $500 for dinner at a four-star restaurant.

It's his contrary nature that causes a passive-aggressive man to demand that things go his way: he wants to go to this movie or that vacation spot; he wants you to dress a certain way; he wants you to agree with him; he wants to feel commanding. If the autocrat doesn't get his way or if you protest, he pouts, punishing you with more passive-aggression.

Since the autocrat shields himself by noninvolvement—being hostile, withdrawn, uncommunicative, sulking in your presence—the key is to get him involved. You should handle this by specifically addressing the situation, leveling with him and tactfully getting to the bottom of what might be driving him. If he reluctantly goes along with the group who vetoed his choice of movie/dinner/other activity and behaves badly or storms off, then you have to clue him in to some ground rules of socially acceptable behavior.

If he's been especially difficult, tell him how he affects others. *Talk about the issue.* ("The point of the evening is being together, not *where* we go on *your* say-so. Ruining the evening for other people is *unacceptable*. And while I love being with you, I'd rather not when you act this way.") Sometimes you can address the issue simply, with a good-natured tone of voice or make an easy-to-take joke of it. ("Well, you got voted down tonight, John. We won't get to see *Robin Hood*, but I'll let you wear some green tights later when we get home.")

If he's still pouting after your attempts to bring him around, acknowledge his feelings, but discourage his pouting from continuing. ("I know you're still upset about this, but it does you no good to sulk, and I don't like it either.") Sometimes it's best to give him a lot of room, if that's what he needs— allow him a few hours to blow off steam.

But if he's pouting about not having gotten his way and it's two days later, you have to talk straight to him. Tell him he's not being mature about it. ("I care about you. Your friends care about you, but you've been unable to make a small concession for us. It was just a movie, not life and death. The movie is still playing, and you're still playing victim over nothing. *Grow up*, John!")

MISSING ACCOUNTABILITY

Let's look at Linda and Rick's situation. After two years of marriage, Linda, a twenty-nine-year-old pediatric nurse, lost her tolerance for her husband Rick's "charming naïveté" as he became more and more careless with her.

First, a small matter: Rick often promised to do the dinner dishes, but he always found more important things to attend to, such as followup business calls. Linda would remind him, and he'd say, "Sure, hon, in a second. . . ." but he'd never get to it. Linda began leaving the dishes until the morning, but Rick was too rushed to do them then; and at dinner, another batch would pile up. Finally, Linda would give up in frustration and do them herself. But catering to passive-aggression is not the road to success.

More critical was Rick's lack of respect for Linda's time and possessions. Whenever they planned a rendezvous, Rick showed up at least fifteen minutes late. No matter how many times she complained, he couldn't get himself to the appointed place on time. Linda chose to take a humorous tack, and one year bought him two watches for his birthday ("so you'll have no excuse for being late"). And while Rick enjoyed the joke, she's still waiting for him.

On one occasion, Rick borrowed her credit card and then failed to return it after repeated requests. He'd begin to go for it, then change the subject or lie, saying he must have left it in the office. When she discovered that he'd lost it weeks before, and confronted him with the fact, he wasn't in the least bit apologetic. "What did it matter?" he asked her. "No one used it illegally." Also, he reminded her, feeling superior, "Think about how much money I saved *you* from spending."

Linda referred to this as the "problem of missing accountability," because there was no one to accept the blame for her lost credit card or the dirty dishes or the time she spent waiting on a street corner. Rick wouldn't admit he'd done something unseemly. He couldn't face it "like a man." Just when she thought Rick would have to admit his guilt, he turned the tables on her, telling her he'd actually done her a favor.

Linda made the decision never to lend her husband anything of value again. This is a tough resolution to keep, since she's a fundamentally trusting person. But Rick forced her to this position. It was the only way to protect herself. He shifted the focus from his violation of her rights to another major interpersonal issue between husband and wife: *trust*. Linda is still troubled about this incident and worried about whether or not she can trust him, or rely on him, in the future.

You may need to make just such a decision.

THE PROBLEM OF ALCOHOLISM

Alcoholism is common among more severely troubled passive-aggressive men, exacerbating the problem of "missing accountability." Many alcoholics don't acknowledge their drinking problem, and some of those who do may not assume responsibility for their actions while inebriated. Most instances of marital violence occur when the husband is drunk; it's the alcohol, such a man thinks, that's doing the violence. Sober, he's apologetic, abject, pleading for forgiveness, even breaking into tears. Drunk, he's out of control.

For whatever the passive-aggressive drinker did or didn't do, he will have a ready excuse: "I was drunk." He may apologize, but the remorse isn't genuine—he doesn't truly accept responsibility for what he did. The basis for his thinking is that he wouldn't have acted badly if he hadn't been drunk. Since he continues to drink, the problem inevitably recurs.

While this *disowning* of one's actions is certainly a passive-aggressive dynamic—as is immersing oneself in consciousness-altering chemicals to bury or change feelings—obviously, any episode of violence would never be labeled "*passive*-aggressive." It's clear, active and direct.

Alcoholism is a complex issue worthy of greater investigation (and requires treatment in programs for alcoholics), but for now, I hope to simply point out its place in the dynamics of some passive-aggressive men—disowning responsibility, avoiding intimacy, fostering conflict.

The contradiction between the man's loving demeanor while sober and his hostile behavior while drunk mirrors the paradox between the passive and aggressive sides of this man's psychology. Wives of alcoholics claim that they are confused and mistrustful of such an inconsistency: Which is the real personality? they wonder. The answer is: *both*.

SOLITUDE

Escape into solitude is another kind of drug.

Marriage to a passive-aggressive man can be a solitary experience, where you feel as if you've been frozen out of his life, emotionally and physically. When you're warm, he's distant; when you need his attention, it's elsewhere. He can coolly shut you out of his innermost thoughts and feelings, failing to respond to your openness, your affection, your humor and your vulnerability. He's a man able to be alone in the company of others, and paradoxically enough, a man afraid to be alone without you.

If the single passive-aggressive man has a gift for using actual distance to protect his feelings from you, the married passive-aggressive man is a master at engineering his own disappearing acts. The need for solitude and privacy are normal desires, but taken to extreme, these demands can be isolationist, unsociable and reflect a sad attempt at self-protection. It is obviously a sign that a marriage is in trouble when his withdrawal is a problem for you.

Josie and Ian's five-year marriage turned into such a remote relationship. The bane of Josie's life was Ian's pattern of sleeping excessively, as much as eleven and twelve hours a day. When Josie took into account the time Ian spent at work, it left very little time for her. She felt lonely and ignored, and it was clear that Ian was using sleep as a means of escape from the intimacy of their marriage.

Josie reluctantly accepted the fact that Ian "needed" this much sleep, but she often wanted to wake him to talk or ask him to do a chore. If she let him sleep, she remained frustrated, and if she woke him, Ian was annoyed. He set up a no-win situation, and Josie complied with it.

Ian is one kind of "unconscious" husband—literally unconscious in his case. There are other ways to disconnect from a marriage. Some passive-aggressive men egocentrically focus on themselves, leaving little time for, and having minimal interest in, other people, including their spouses. Others become overly preoccupied with careers or overinvolved in leisure activities, to the exclusion of honoring a sense of partnership. Mounting outside interests leave a wife to lead her own life, and, if she cares about her husband and the marriage, it's a guarantee of loneliness.

A man who prefers to watch a television program that makes no real difference in his life, for example, rather than deal with a wife who needs him, both denigrates and abandons her. Wives who complain to their husbands about such an insult leave themselves open to further rejection. It's a double bind: some wives continue trying to break through to their detached spouses; others, at some point along the way, implicitly accept the situation and the solitude their marriage has brought.

The passive-aggressive man who retreats into solitude often experiences a two-sided conflict. He wants to declare how independent he is by being the loner, even if it means being unconscious, but his declaration is usually made to the very person he feels *dependent on.*

Since this guy sees your attempts to reach him as a ploy to trap him into a state of togetherness that he's not ready for, like Josie, you have to figure out what he's feeling. If you let him alone (because he says he has work to do or he wants some privacy or he's tired and wants to sleep) or you let him be (because he's sulking in the next room), in truth, he may really want contact. The problem arises because he can't admit this to himself or to you. Instead, he's annoyed or hurt, thinking you've rejected him.

In classic passive-aggressive style, he's created a double bind: leave him alone, and he feels you don't care about him; approach him, and he feels you're too demanding. To find a solution with the loner, you have to walk a fine line and discover what it is he wants.

If, like Josie, you feel that you're leading parallel lives under one roof, you need to communicate about what's really happening in your husband's life (pressures about work; with children from another marriage; from his parents) and begin making adjustments. Marriage goes through phases— downswings when you're not getting along and you doubt your feelings for each other. Is withdrawal a symptom of this down trend or the style in which he relates?

Once you know that, you can proceed.

While you want to coax him into greater involvement in the relationship, remember that he's entitled to privacy and freedom. As are you. Be honest. Tell him what you'd like—dinner together at least four nights a week, which weekend day you want to spend with him and how long, etc., and emphasize how much you miss being with him.

The relationship is yours jointly, to benefit both of you. Stress this. Bring up what the relationship means to you, and ask him what he thinks is missing. ("I want our marriage to work. Is there something I'm not doing that you need? I feel that you're avoiding me much of the time.") It's likely he'll respond and give you, if not fully intimate revelations, at least some idea of what's bothering him. Progress like this is incremental and gradual.

Your best bet with an isolationist is not to demand more than he's freely willing to give; a tiny step forward into your life is better than a closed door. His terms may not be acceptable to you—but this passive-aggressive man doesn't want to feel obligated to you. If any man can give you a sense that yours is a *voluntary* relationship, easily severed, it is he.

WORKING THINGS OUT

The problems facing all the couples in this chapter are really metaphors for a greater issue. Although the people involved have made a public and private commitment to each other, *they do not deal with each other as committed allies in a fully trusting way*. They are not true partners.

In a partnership, you're both on the same side, even when there are disagreements and fights. Two people are never going to think alike. And for marriage, or any close relationship, to work, it must be a partnership that can tolerate disagreement and conflict, so you can reunite with a purpose. A good marriage isn't about the absence of fighting. Once you're in opposite corners, there will be a moment when you don't know who is going to initiate peace and how—but the *sine qua non* of any good relationship is the ability and capacity to move through the process of conflict and recognize that your interests are aligned.

Since unity of purpose and clarity of motives are intrinsic to good partnerships, you'll need to examine the topography of your relationship. Are you making yourself clear to your spouse about what you want and how you feel or are you hesitant about revealing yourself? Is it a situation where he's simply *entitled* to his freedom, and you feel he's being passive-aggressive because he's *not giving you what you want*? If you think you're reasonable, and that he *is* a passive-aggressive mate, then you'll have to make the first moves to change the dynamic between you to get out of your downward spiral.

Once there's been a disagreement, a passive-aggressive spouse will feel he's failing you, making him all the more angry and ashamed—he made a promise, he broke it, you pointed it out, he defended himself and added an offhand but rude enough barb about you; you took exception and retaliated; he escalated the battle and so on. *You will need to prove that you're on his side* by letting him know that his interests are your interests, his battles are your battles.

Some passive-aggressive men cherish family bonds but still behave as if they have no one to answer to but themselves and tip the balance toward discord, not accord. Others feel lashed to family bonds rather than happily bonded to family, and wind up leaving. In any case, with a committed relationship—whether you're living together or married, the stakes are raised for the success of the relationship—he doesn't want to lose you or his children. The man who fears abandonment the most will make the greatest effort at keeping the relationship going, but his efforts may fall short of what you need.

The married couple who can duke it out are also able to talk through their problems. ("I'm angry because you did this . . . you didn't do that. . . .") Relationships improve when you develop skills that productively help you out of conflicts. The passive-aggressive man needs help articulating what he's unhappy about; once you learn what it is, you both can start to figure out some compromise that's suitable for each of you.

WHAT IF NO APPROACH WORKS?

A lot of relationships can change, but some will not—that is the bad news. Your decision may be that closing a door makes more sense to you than always having to knock on it to see if your passive-aggressive spouse is in or out. Leaving, sometimes, is your only solution. If, over the years, most of your energy is expended on short-lived and essentially ineffective repairs to the relationship, rather than living the relationship with its pleasures and pains, it may be time to get out.

At a certain point, you have to recognize that your interests will be trampled on. If your relationship is about how-your-relationship-doesn't-work, and you see no improvement, then your healthiest move may be to end it. You are entitled to more, and if the passive-aggressive in your life cannot or will not give it, seek your happiness elsewhere. Again, it means sizing up the situation realistically—knowing what he does and does not give to the relationship, assessing the real value of his promises to change.

THE PASSIVE-AGGRESSIVE FAMILY MAN

The passive-aggressive man doesn't fundamentally change when he becomes a father. The intensity of emotion for him in the relationship with his children is as great as with any family member. Fatherhood places additional burdens on him, and he may even engage in a subtle or open competition with his infant child for his wife's affection and attention. As a father, he can be just as sensitive to the demands and expectations placed on him and resist them, often as strongly as he does with a wife or a boss. To some degree, his conflicts about being a parent mirror the problems he had with his own father.

His solitude and stinginess—not necessarily with money as much as with affection and attention—can have a very negative impact on his children. He wants to be a good father but he often doesn't spend adequate time with his children and resents their demands on him—demands that any normal child would make. His ambivalent feelings reassert themselves. He wants to be a good father, but he hopes you, his wife, will take over as the main provider of attention and affection. Since he feels guilty about not being a good father—in part, by leaving most of the responsibility to you—he withdraws further.

Let's take a closer look.

TAKING CHARGE

The most difficult aspect of parenting for the passive-aggressive man is *disciplining his children*. While he may assume the position of authority ("It's my house and you do as I say"), set rules and teach the difference between right and wrong, he falls short of being the "enforcer."

Most passive-aggressive men don't like to play the heavy, preferring to hand the job over to you. Since it's natural for children to test the limits of their parents' patience, at some point we are all forced to take a stand. The passive-aggressive man tries to evade this crisis point, hoping the child will change before he's forced to confront him. It's a form of procrastination that keeps a passive-aggressive father feeling safe from his children's wrath—although they're bound to keep fighting, since children are hungry for just such an authority figure.

One "benign" personality, Eric, reacts with a sense of confusion or fright when his daughter, Regina, cries, or worse, throws a tantrum. Eric's wife always jumps to take over and soothe her, to his relief. Regina, in her innocence, knows how to manipulate her father and get her way with him simply by fussing or threatening to carry on. The following "dress incident" shows how.

When her birthday was coming up, her parents bought six-year-old Regina a new dress, which they stored away in a secret location out of her reach. Eric told me:

When my wife was out one afternoon, I heard Regina tearing through her closet and then my wife's closet, in search of the dress. I knew she wanted to try it on. However, I also knew that if the dress was messed up for the party, my wife would be furious.

So when Regina came in to ask me where it was, I couldn't tell her what she already knew: *You cannot try on the dress. It's special for next week.* Instead, I lied to her. I wanted to get away from the subject so I said, "What dress? I don't know about any birthday dress for you. Ask your mother."

This response confused Regina, who remembered telling him about the dress when it was bought. Eric, maintaining a casual air, and needing to forestall a tantrum, insisted, "I can't remember all your clothes. Go play in your room," and resumed reading his paper.

Many parents opt for *denial* to avoid dealing with an issue they aren't emotionally prepared for at the moment. For Eric, simply asserting to his daughter the limitations about wearing her party dress brings up conflicts about himself as a good father. Afraid of his child's potential anger, he automatically froze.

To feel threatened by a child—and give her such power over him—is a striking example of how out of kilter Eric's perceptions are. Such unnecessary lies confuse children—they don't understand which reality to trust—theirs or his. They begin to act out more, pushing limits just to get a rise out of a father like this.

Certain other passive-aggressive fathers take out their frustration with authority figures (bosses, colleagues who have surer footing and clearer road maps up the success track) on the people in their lives who are least able to defend themselves: their children. Psychologists have a name for this process of transferring to others the feeling of being downtrodden, taken advantage of or abused: "identification with the aggressor." They strike back. Since they feel mistreated, they believe they're entitled to mistreat others. Although passive-aggressive fathers are not likely to beat their children, they're capable of causing excessive psychological pressure and meting out punishments that do not "fit the crime."

Lars is an example of a passive-aggressive father who really pushes his daughters hard. An angry man who won't own up to it, Lars makes them feel unloved and barely tolerated, born an unfortunate accident of fate. He often makes excessive demands on them regarding household chores: "*Earn your keep*," he tells them, adding more and more things for them to do. Rather than making his children feel valued, this Machiavellian father uses his power to abuse them.

For the passive-aggressive father on such a warpath, a child can do no right. He will demean a child who's doing poorly in school, telling him that he's incapable of learning, reinforcing the child's worst fears. He sets standards for his children, but ups the ante if these standards *are* met. Meanwhile, he holds himself up to them as flawless, loving and always right. It reflects a contradiction between the "caring" father who is looking out for his daughters' best interests, pushing them to do ever better, and the abusive father who pulls the rug out from under them anytime they have reason to feel proud of themselves.

Although family life is the source of the greatest love and support in the life of a passive-aggressive man, it can be a sore spot inspiring most of his contrary behavior. He may look for signs of too many pressures, and count the inadvertent slights, which he can't overlook or easily forgive. The family life he will create with you may begin to recapitulate his early family life, stirring the memories and conflicts from his often unhappy childhood.

Can he change? What can you bring to the relationship to deflect some of these old issues for him? The following guidelines can give you some direction for strengthening your marriage.

HELPING YOUR HUSBAND HANDLE FATHERHOOD

The passive-aggressive father finds it difficult to assume the role of father, role model, authority and boss, although he loves the idea of himself as the person in charge. The problem focuses on a lack of knowledge about dealing with children, an unwillingness to bear the brunt of discord and anger if things go wrong and the inability to own up that "the buck stops here."

Knowledge is easiest to handle and can pave the way toward your best solution. Though thousands of books have been written about raising children and how to wisely handle their unique problems, the passive-aggressive man probably hasn't read one of them. He wants to raise his children his way—but his style is filtered through his passive-aggression and distorts its effectiveness.

A child's experience of the world pretty much comes from his parents. They're a child's source of love, limits, games, developing conscience, self-esteem. The passive-aggressive father may not have the skills to handle a small child's uncensored emotions, questions and demands, and, conversely, he may not want to admit what he doesn't know. Instead, he appears to run away from the role of father or evade issues with his children as they come up.

Since no man wants to be a lousy father, it will be up to you, his wife, to help him assume a stronger role by *gently* giving him advice about dealing with children. Tell him what to expect ("Four-year-olds go through a testing period, and since they can talk, they're a bit more trouble than two-year-olds."), and how to manage the child and the situation. *He'll be proud of himself when the kids respond favorably.* Helpful information and compliments ("You were great with the kids at the pool, Jack!") perpetuate positive cycles. Remember, the passive-aggressive family man did not have an adequate paternal role model. He needs encouragement and support to find his way. ("Now, Jack . . . your father may not have done it this way, but you can.") And the motto "the buck stops here" makes sense only if you've had the experience yourself.

Many passive-aggressive fathers make promises to their children that they have no intention of keeping. Don't just stand by and watch this drama of disappointment play itself out. Intervene in a tactful way. ("Now, Bill, it's unrealistic to think you'll be back from the club in time for Jennifer's dance class. Why don't you cancel your golf game?") It's better for the kids, and it's better for Bill.

IN CLOSING . . .

The influence of intimate and childhood relationships is remarkably powerful in an individual's life. Particular patterns of interaction persist into adulthood for, really, no rational reason. The passive-aggressive man still rails against many unresolved feelings from his past, sometimes to no avail and at other times with a fair degree of success in the relationship he forms with you.

He also faces his destiny in the outside world, where forgiveness doesn't come to him as easily, and his actions alone are all that count. In the next chapter, you'll get to understand how the passive-aggressive man deals with his second great conflict: competition and work.

10

THE MINE FIELD: THE PASSIVE-AGGRESSIVE MAN AT WORK

THE PASSIVE-AGGRESSIVE MAN at work is a master of intrigue and control. He's resourceful and smart, devious and complicated. He plans, he plots, he knows what must be done to succeed. And if you're his colleague, you're just a pawn in his game. He wants you to believe his is not a selfish quest; by praising your competence and appearing to promote your career, he convinces you that he's on your side. But then the gambit unfolds, and you wonder why you fell for his story.

Shakespeare's Iago, foe of Othello, is such a schemer who deftly and surreptitiously controls the people around him. He is completely manipulative, selfish and unfeeling, and his skill lies in never revealing his true nature. His feelings are always held in check, hidden behind a mask, though he tells just enough of the truth to be believable. The audience alone is aware of Iago's scheme, while those around him unwittingly act as his agents and succumb to his grand plan. Iago never drops the guise of loyal soldier to his king, even at those moments when he lies to and betrays him. Iago is the consummate passive-aggressive man at the peak of his powers.

Since passive-aggression is fundamentally about power and control, it's not surprising that the passive-aggressive man constantly gets into power struggles at work. He doesn't so much act the top sergeant, barking commands, as he plays it covertly, coolly and brilliantly. The Iago-at-work sets you up to do the work and take the fall for him, controlling your behavior until you feel like a puppet on his string.

Like Iago acting behind the scenes, he lays traps that you unsuspectingly stumble into. Even when you see them, there seems to be no way to avoid them. Once again you say to yourself, *Why am I doing this? How did I get into this mess? Why am I carrying out his agenda and sacrificing my own?*

Other passive-aggressive men are just as devious and complicated as Iago, but much less resourceful and far more self-defeating. He may think he's on a success track, but he derails himself more often than not. He's full of tricks that have no effect or that backfire, so he either is fired or is not promoted. He's the guy who plots *in his dreams*, but demonstrates little or no real initiative on the job.

Passive-aggression is the stuff of typical business days, everywhere. You are undoubtably familiar with it. Passive-aggressive men want to succeed; *you* want them to succeed, but every one of them makes chinks in his own armor. As he is emotionally impaired, so may he be professionally impaired in a number of ways that may, however, be correctable. Let's take a look at how.

PASSIVE-AGGRESSION AT WORK: WHAT'S IT ALL ABOUT?

The guy who has to be reminded to ask for a raise and pushed to assert himself or the man who is so insecure that he keeps a tight stranglehold over the workplace is rarely heading toward success. Rather, he reflects another major conflict churning in passive-aggressive men—the *conflict over competition*.

Competition and striving for success stir up our aggressive impulses. While normally these are held in check or channeled in useful ways, the passive-aggressive man is tied up in knots—afraid that others will retaliate, and guilt-ridden should they not. This is clearly indicative of neurotic conflict, since most men are fairly comfortable with competition.

The passive-aggressive man makes a faulty connection between aggression, assertion, action and anger, confusing them and turning them into a single concept in his mind. Direct confrontation causes trouble—since someone may get hurt, he decides to compete less directly. By being *passively* competitive, he thinks he's less threatening, a "good guy." Unfortunately, his indirectness is counterproductive for all concerned.

Passive-aggressive men are afraid of direct competition in a number of ways. Some of them love the idea of success but hate having won it—they'll manage to sabotage themselves somehow. They avoid the spotlight, yet resent when others have it; they're overwhelmed by taking charge and the pressures that come from being the chief decision maker. But they're equally unable to do as they're told. Some men seek out failure—by being unable to make or close a deal, by missing meetings, antagonizing prospects, etc.—appearing to find comfort more by having lost than having won. In all such passive-aggressive men, it is their discomfort with competition and achievement that intrigues psychoanalysts: What dynamic could possibly explain a seemingly unnatural pull to undermine one's own success?

Problems involving competition with all other men are an outgrowth of an unresolved, traditional Oedipus conflict. To a passive-aggressive man, competition is interpreted within the framework of *rivalry* with his father. To succeed means to vanquish his father, a condition he finds emotionally unacceptable, engendering tremendous guilt in him. Of course, to *lose* is also unacceptable and creates in him an equal amount of resentment and fear.

Caught between the two "evils"—intolerable success and

intolerable failure—a passive-aggressive man solves the problem by *withdrawing* from competition. It's as if he says, "You see, Dad, I'm no threat." It's a throwback to his childhood when he wanted to win to gain his father's approval as a male, but he feared winning since he'd undermine or usurp his father's authority and lose his love.

The inertia and indecisiveness of passive-aggression provide an inadequate resolution to this old issue for men. As long as the passive-aggressive man thinks of himself as non-threatening, he can never acknowledge his true feelings or bring his conflict over competition to a satisfactory psychological resolution in guilt-free assertiveness and ambition, that is, in a sense, to untie his hands and unleash his competitive drives.

Achievement and productivity are about moving forward, overcoming obstacles, making sure that one's efforts pay off. The hung-up passive-aggressive man feels his efforts can't make a difference, so he doesn't bother trying. He spins his wheels when he needs to engage the clutch and make progress, even if only a little at a time. Helping him to direct his energies in a productive way improves his self-image and further motivates him.

A passive-aggressive man to one degree or another plays out his conflicts over competition at work from either side: as boss or as employee. Whether you work for a passive-aggressive boss or have to manage a passive-aggressive employee, this trait in action is particularly frustrating. Here's how.

PERSISTENT EXCUSE MAKING

The passive-aggressive man's approach to doing business puts him in the unenviable position of having to explain his motives and failures—frequently. Since he perceives himself as never at fault, he puts the responsibility elsewhere, through blame or excuse making. And he does it with considerable panache.

Some of his excuses can be quite inventive and convincing, until you learn differently. Since he's so self-protective, he makes the kind of excuses that absolve *him* and blame you. He'll sacrifice you to get out of a commitment if he has to. For example, he might cancel out of an appointment at the last minute—or not show up at all—creating a false sense of urgency over a nonexistent event.

Excuses for why he did not show up/complete what he started/clinch the deal may ring true. ("I know I'm late; my engine conked out on me ten minutes from the office. . . ." "Four-thirty this morning, I'm awakened by a leak in the ceiling. It took hours to get a plumber and roofer over. . . .") Such excuses may have been true once, but you will hear them more than once, or a variation of them in a month or two when again he falls short of doing his job.

Other excuses for not doing his work are plain childish. ("Who can work for a bureaucrat and get anything done?" "This office is impossible; the phone never stops ringing. . . ." or "I'd have done the job if you'd have left me alone.") The more manipulative the man, the more often he'll make excuses: "I forgot my appointment book" (for the tenth time). If you don't accept his excuses at face value, then you'll be the one at fault. He'll accuse *you* of being unfair or inconsiderate or taking something out of context. As before, whether he's being boyish and placating or challenging and haughty, this is the problem of missing accountability.

If a passive-aggressive man put as much creativity and effort into actual accomplishment as he does into making up excuses—whether in his relationships or at work—he'd achieve the power he yearns for. But he'll only have power when he learns to assume responsibility for his setbacks, shortcomings and failures, and learns to change them. Until then, his excuses may get you off his back but will keep him in the same place.

There is only one way to contain a compulsive excuse maker: hold him accountable for what he does and doesn't do. This is what we mean by setting limits.

OBSTRUCTIONISM: SETTING UP A MAZE OF BARRIERS

In endeavors that need cooperation and compatibility, a passive-aggressive man may choose to work covertly to sabotage and undermine what you do. He may even sacrifice his own productivity to bring you down with him. Being his partner is next to impossible under these terms. The passive-aggressive man and you become adversaries, when you should be allies. Disagreements may not surface openly, but every basis for cooperation will be challenged in an unacknowledged war of wills.

The obstructionist's style is strangely paradoxical. He's unwilling to display leadership, but he's also unwilling to relinquish control to others. Passivity and manipulating others are his calling cards; they're how he asserts himself. Nevertheless, he's just as controlling as the openly domineering personality.

Despite appearances and the lavish promises he may make, the passive-aggressive man is a destructive presence at work, fostering power struggles, encouraging standoffs and complaints and leaving issues unresolved. He seeks out areas of tension and then exacerbates them. His behavior serves as a constant reminder that problems exist. If you're a Rescuer, you'll be pulling the obstructionist out of ruts too often; and if you are a Manager, a woman who "can't take no for an answer," you'll be on guard as he tests your power every day. Meanwhile, mistrust flourishes.

Rather than work as a facilitator, a passive-aggressive man creates more obstacles and difficulties than he breaks through. When it comes to throwing a monkey wrench into plans, he's got perfect aim.

Obstructionism takes many forms. A legislator filibusters to delay action over a congressional bill; a union stages a work slowdown; someone stubbornly holds to an opinion despite overwhelming evidence to the contrary and causes unnecessary delays. Obstructionism can be blatant or subtle and have a specific aim or a vague, scattershot intent, underhanded and pointless. Whatever its form, the passive-aggressive man's negative and contrary style makes his presence felt.

As soon as you seek his cooperation, you become hooked into his passive-aggressive games, because now he has leverage. He can obstruct whatever you want to accomplish. Obstructionism can be especially ferocious when it is the style of your boss. Kathy's case shows how.

After a year as senior programmer for a computer company, Kathy was assigned to a different division widely known as a graveyard for budding careers. She soon found out why: the division head, Simon. Her first impression of him was as affable, welcoming and eager to work cooperatively. However, he was easily threatened by bright and ambitious underlings or colleagues, especially women. Rather than be a mentor to these junior executives, Simon plotted to derail them.

Among his many ploys, Simon would withhold crucial programming information from Kathy that would have facilitated her productivity. If Kathy showed initiative on a particular project, Simon would first give his tacit approval and then undermine her every step of the way. He'd ask her to rewrite or revise her work countless times, and usually by the sixth rewrite, he'd *return to the first draft*. He'd hire people for a special project but not allocate enough office space or phone lines. He destroyed creativity and demoralized the staff.

Kathy reacted as any normal person would. She doubted her skills (with Simon as her judge), and lost interest in the project, putting it aside because she was unsure of what Simon wanted. The coup de grace would come when he innocently asked her one day, "Where's that programming project?" or "Can't I count on you to get things done?" This was when Kathy realized she was being manipulated, and it made her angry. But again, as an underling, she had neither the means nor authority to retaliate or deal with Simon's problem constructively.

One of Simon's most hostile maneuvers was to create as

much anxiety as possible among his staff, and then offer no reassurance. Kathy told me:

> Simon really knew how to make me and two other junior executives feel insecure.
>
> He'd want us to believe that some catastrophe over which we had no control was about to erupt—anything from layoffs to job redefinition to no bonuses. All of us would begin to worry—the "crisis" was our chief topic of conversation. We would go around and around in circles, worked up. Then things would cool down a week or two later.
>
> Afterward, we tracked down the "crisis" and discovered that Simon knew what was going on all along and had had the information to allay our fears for most of that time. He kept it to himself, though, and let us worry. No one enjoys others' insecurity more than him.

If you're at the mercy of a man like Simon, you wonder why he behaves as he does and what he gets from taking the joy from work and making others miserable. Scrutinize such obstructionism and we'll find it is a recapitulation of a childhood pattern with one important difference—whereas before he felt he had no power over his life, now he can reverse the role and make you feel that you have no power over yours. By doing unto others what was done to him as a child, Simon feels he has mastered his earlier anxieties.

Other ways Simon displayed his obstructionism was to "damn with faint praise." Grudging praise does more harm than good. And since he channeled most of his energy and competitive drive into sabotaging others, he had little fuel left for his own achievements. It's a common pattern for the passive-aggressive man at work to undermine others and do nothing to further himself.

Why would a company keep a man who was counterproductive to their needs? Inertia. As division chief, Simon had reached the pinnacle of his career advancement—the company CEO knew Simon's work was mediocre; he was someone who would neither be promoted nor fired. But corporate inertia has its costs. Since his own professional life was stagnant, Simon couldn't bear to have anyone around him to stir up the waters and outdistance him. So he did what he could to get what glory was left for him.

There's always the feeling that you're up against the wall when you work with the obstructionist. Since your frustration level is always being tested by him, do what you can to clear a wide path away from him. Your best move is to unlink your efforts, and especially your advancement, with his. Try to minimize the effects of his obstructionism on you. Stand up to his ruses, *name his game*, and tell him you know what he's up to. In a calm tone, offer him another chance, tell him he's valuable to the project, but that you will not jump over his blockades any longer. If this doesn't succeed, then work around him, and if you must, work without him.

SCREWING UP

The epitome of the "screwup" is actually a woman, not a man: the sexist stereotype of the ditzy secretary. It's a common enough character sketch: the secretary smiles sweetly, but ask her to do something and she can't get it right. She can never find the phone number you need, the file that will answer your questions; ask her to type something, and misspellings and omissions are guaranteed. When you're in a rush, she takes extended coffee breaks or makes personal phone calls. A cup of coffee accidentally spills on an important paper; when you are in a most sensitive situation with a client, she's got an inappropriate remark for the occasion, delivered with what she believes is real charm. And when you have to count on her, she's out sick.

Whether male or female, secretary or assistant, the stereotype holds true. When the ditzy secretary makes a mistake, she apologizes profusely. However, you notice that she fails to learn from her mistakes—she *still* loses files and can't be counted on. She plays deaf, dumb and blind when you ask her to do something. She is a passive listener who stubbornly refuses to ask the necessary questions to understand your directions or instructions. She stares at you blankly, and then goes happily forward without seeking clarification, although she has no idea what you want. Ask her if she understands, and she'll swear that she does. But when she turns in her work, it's clear she was following instructions from another planet.

Keeping things ambiguous is convenient: it offers her an excuse for not meeting responsibilities or expectations, such as, "I didn't realize you wanted *this* and not *that*," or, more provocatively, "Why didn't you tell me what you wanted in the first place?" This behavior may become so frustrating for you that eventually you cave in and swear, "I'd rather do it myself," a solution that does little good since it only doubles your work load.

The prototype of the inefficient secretary, whom you may have to fire eventually to save your business, captures the essence of the passive-aggressive screwup, man or woman. When a passive-aggressive man undermines himself, as does the maddeningly inefficient secretary, he undermines you in the process. These screwups are not accidental— they are expressions of hostility and should be dealt with that way.

Take Howard, who started screwing up with consistency after being passed over for promotion a few times. A thirty-two-year-old accountant, Howard has been at a large accounting firm for seven years. Ben, his supervisor, regularly gave him constructive feedback about his performance, but Howard wasn't changing.

When Ben assigned him and two other accountants to work on an important project, Howard scowled, making his displeasure obvious to everyone. Ben ignored it because he was not about to negotiate with Howard about which tasks he would and wouldn't perform and with whom. He assumed Howard was a grown-up and a team player and would do his job. As it turned out, it was misplaced optimism.

Right from the start, Howard proved difficult to get along

with: he skipped meetings, broke appointments, didn't do his share of the work, and when he did, it was usually incomplete and poorly done. His excuses for *why* his work was inadequate were flimsy and foolish, and eventually Howard no longer bothered to offer an excuse. Instead, he stopped showing up, missing days of work due to "illness."

Howard's foot-dragging and absenteeism didn't sit well with his co-workers, one of whom is a patient of mine. Patty told me:

> We complained to Ben that we wanted Howard off the project. He was impossible. We preferred to take on his share of the job rather than deal with his mistakes. We couldn't get the guy to do anything right, and we were his friends.

Patty's complaints finally hit home with Ben, who'd avoided dealing with the "Howard situation" for too long. Ben had always thought of him as "deadwood," but now he realized something worse: Howard damaged the morale of the entire division, and hobbled the effectiveness of the other workers. He couldn't let it go any longer.

At this point, Ben belatedly confronted the problem of how to deal with a passive-aggressive man at work. He knew that constructive criticism was hopeless, and a speech about "shaping up or shipping out" would only exacerbate an already uncomfortable situation. Ben either had to fire Howard (in effect, giving up on him) or accept him as he was, because Howard was certainly never going to leave voluntarily. So Ben decided to fire him, although with great misgivings (even Patty felt guilty when her ne'er-do-well colleague was fired).

In general, the passive-aggressive employee is a real challenge for a manager, and such behavior is much less tolerated at work than at home. It's easier to set limits, give ultimatums, talk straight when you aren't personally involved. Ben's mistake was not facing up to the "Howard problem" sooner. He should never have tolerated deadwood, and the minute he detected Howard's disgruntlement, he should have confronted him. Don't ignore the early warning signals.

While the average person is motivated by pride and sense of accomplishment, the passive-aggressive man at his most self-destructive shows no such pride in achievement. On the contrary, he has a remarkable capacity to tolerate incompleteness and incompetence. If he messes up, it's because of that ambivalence about achievement and productivity. He takes two steps back for every three steps forward, sometimes, sadly, undermining *prior* achievements, rejecting support and prematurely cutting off gratifying results. When things are going at a clip, he pulls back and grinds to a halt. Like Howard, he undoes progress. It's not that he likes to screw up and goof off; it's that he's anxious and angry. This is a classic case of what is meant by "fear of success."

I've discovered that men who hit such peaks of nonproductivity have, in part, a different sense of time from you and me. The screwup squanders time. Normally, impatience motivates us to make a change, even reluctantly, but the passive-aggressive man waits for change to come to him—and he may resent it and resist it when it does. Unfortunately, while he's waiting, he may diminish the value of real opportunities, and pass them by, never to recover them.

If you work with a "Howard," try not to get caught up in the details of his screw-ups or try to "fix" things for him. Cover your trail at all times by documenting what you've done—send daily memos to your boss, if you have to. You need to protect yourself from a Howard. If he's a marginal case, give him the benefit of the doubt. Compliment him on what he does well (if he's still working there, he must be functioning in some capacity), and reassure him if he's afraid. If you're Howard's boss, give him a series of short assignments, each with an absolute deadline. Don't lower your standards or extend the deadline. If he doesn't come through, you, like Ben, may have to fire him. You can't let his anger interfere with your productivity or the work environment in general.

ON THE INSULT TRAIN

Since he is self-absorbed, a passive-aggressive man is often inadvertently insulting and overbearing. He's as likely as not to say something bitingly mean and sarcastic without ever recognizing the impact of his remarks. Others, meanwhile, never really know what he thinks.

He needs to be important and *pursued*, and this leads him to concoct a number of ongoing crazy-making games. For example, some executives who play phone games may use their secretaries to continually interrupt meetings or cut them short with "urgent" messages. Such interruptions are to remind the visitor that the executive has other more pressing obligations—an implicit insult.

Although the urgent-message ploy is an accepted business practice, taken for granted in many circles and intended to make an executive appear successful and busy, it's still passive-aggression. Most of all, the executive hopes to communicate that he's more powerful than you and in control. Such petty jibes can't help but irritate whoever is on the receiving end.

A patient of mine, Ellen, told me a tale about her boss. Napoleonic in style, the man almost never complimented his employees or colleagues and tended to take over meetings and negotiations with clients.

Ellen gained some clear insights into her boss's personality when she submitted a proposal for a new product line to be marketed under her direction. Ellen was surprised by his written response: "Great idea!" Considering how sparingly he gave positive feedback, Ellen thought she'd finally made an impression on him until she got to the P.S. in the memo: *"I'll assign Darren to head up the line."* Ellen was dumbfounded by the mixed message—first he acknowledged her ingenuity, then he stripped her of power.

Later, when Ellen brought the subject up, her boss pretended that it never crossed his mind that she wanted to lead the project she created. Evidently, he couldn't pay her the compliment of acknowledging her ability. Instead, his behavior demoralized her. For Ellen, this backhanded compliment was a painful exercise in passive-aggression. All she could do was swallow it.

REFUSING TO MAKE DECISIONS

For the passive-aggressive man to make a stand with conviction and commitment is extremely difficult. Inclined to walk the fine line down the middle, he'll agree when he's alone with you but side with your adversaries when he's with them. If all of you are in the same room and must take a vote about an issue, count on the passive-aggressive man to be the last to cast his ballot. Most likely he'll even then get off the hook by giving a speech about the beauty of "compromise."

Such an indecisive man will have a difficult time dealing with people in certain sensitive situations: firing staff, for one. He hates to be the "bad guy." Mike, a passive-aggressive middle manager at an insurance company, once told me:

> Rather than fire someone, I let the guy *twist in the wind.* It's easier to *make the guy go.* I apply pressure. I push the guy around a lot of the time. I make sure he's not asked to a meeting and that he's told about it. . . .

Mike deals in a convoluted logic where it's easier, or more merciful, to let the employee figure out he's not wanted than to fire him directly, amicably and cleanly. "Termination" is a *direct* expression of hostility, and it makes Mike feel too uncomfortable.

Mike believes that his approach dupes the employee into thinking he's made his own decision to quit, protecting Mike from confrontation or conflict. At most, the employee could accuse him of not being supportive—a crime of omission.

If anything, this indirect approach ends up being more sadistic since uncertainty is dragged out and pressure is exerted over a longer period of time. Worse, the employee hopes for a reprieve, a new chance to prove himself.

Since he's the guy most likely to freeze when you need someone to act fast and wisely, don't rely on this man in a crisis, or in a pinch. Don't give him final say. He's not a leader, so don't ask it of him.

PASSING THE BUCK

When he can't take responsibility for his actions, the passive-aggressive man is likely to click into another of his game-playing modes: buck-passing, a game at which he is a champion. He'll trick an unsuspecting co-worker or underling into holding the bag. If a colleague's suggestion is a success, he takes credit for it; if the idea fails, then he's on record for having doubted it—he's the first to bail out. Buck-passing is not owning up—it is slippery, evasive, cowardly and dishonest.

The buck-passer forgoes simple rules of ethics, letting someone else unjustly suffer the consequences, usually shifting the blame for what went wrong on to someone less powerful than he. Others become his inadvertent victims. Why does he do it? Because the idea of punishment is intolerable to the buck-passer, a sign of his impotence. He can't stand up to authority, fight it out "man to man," and he won't take his punishment "like a man."

Diane's story pretty much describes the passive-aggressive buck-passer's game. Brought in as an executive at a commercial real estate company, Diane thought she had lucked out with Brad, a co-worker on her level. Charming, seemingly cooperative and very gregarious, he wooed Diane at first with visions of what a great team they'd make. Both pitched a huge shopping complex, but the investors pulled out and the deal fell through. Brad's true colors soon shone brightly. Brad quickly told their boss that Diane hadn't done all she could have. Diane said:

When my boss came down hard on me, I confronted Brad, but he refused to take any responsibility. He dared to say, *"But don't you remember, Diane. It was your idea to structure the deal that way, not mine."* I was shocked. What a lie, for one; secondly, if Brad thought I did a poor business plan, he should have said so before we presented it to the investors.

From that day on, I knew I couldn't trust him.

Diane resolved to keep written notes of all their conversations, sending memos to their boss describing in explicit detail the allocation of responsibility on joint projects. When a question arose, Diane referred back to these notes and memos. Although it went against her character to be this suspicious and vigilant, she saw her future in this company and refused to let Brad ruin things for her. Such caution successfully contained Brad's passive-aggression. Once Diane identified him as an adversary, she could deal with him at work.

You will only have satisfaction in your dealings with a buck-passer if you force him to admit what he's doing or prove it—as did Diane. Direct confrontation brings the hostility out in the open and gives you a chance to protect yourself.

THE PERENNIAL SHORTCUT

Even when a passive-aggressive man is given a goal or sets one himself, he can take off into blue-sky territory. A dreamer who's good at spinning tales and believing them, he clings to unrealistic ideas about accomplishing what he sets out to do. He doesn't like "getting bogged down in the mundane details" of life; yet he can just as easily focus on irrelevancies so that nothing is accomplished, and then give up in frustration.

Pointless lists and unnecessary phone calls, for example, convince him he's making great progress. Not unlike the insulting narcissist previously mentioned, a passive-aggressive man wishes he were above it all, that he was singled out so the requirements would be different for him. He's a man who loves shortcuts and easy answers. Unfortunately, this can lead to another problem, procrastination.

A patient once told me about a dream he had in which he wanted to buy something at a store, but was upset to find too many people waiting in line. Since Anthony didn't have the patience to wait, he stepped into a shorter line. Unfortunately, he had no idea what the shorter line was for. Anthony's impatience about standing in line shows a bit of a grandiose attitude—as if he were entitled to special advantages. It's a sense of entitlement that set up unrealistic hopes and led to inevitable disappointment when he discovered that the shorter line didn't go where he wanted it to.

As his dream revealed, shortcuts don't necessarily lead to solutions. While most people will choose the shorter route, the most labor-saving device, the fastest food when in a hurry, Anthony sought them out mindlessly, even when they turned out to be more, rather than less, time-consuming.

A passive-aggressive man needs to understand that to accomplish a goal, he needs to take care of the mundane details, not put them off, fob them off on someone else, or vainly hope *another* route gets him there faster. To get to the head of the line, he must wait or strategically work his way through obstacles. By facing the facts squarely, he will ultimately reach his destination.

WHEN A PASSIVE-AGGRESSIVE MAN WORKS FOR A WOMAN

Women executives whom I interviewed in an informal survey felt they were the object of *more* passive-aggression by subordinates than their male counterparts. This is an intriguing observation. When I asked how, they said their authority was questioned and tested repeatedly, and only after they established absolute limits did the power struggles simmer down. In contrast, they felt male executives (at the same level) got warmer welcomes and were more easily accepted as deal makers, decision makers and authority figures. These same women also reported that male employees were more resentful and contrary toward them than were the women who worked for them.

Why would a passive-aggressive man be more passive-aggressive with a female than with a male boss? The answer is tied to his memory of his mother as overly controlling and his father as absent or weak. He is easily threatened by the dominating presence of a powerful woman, but this same quality reassures him when it's packaged in a man.

Basically, he wants men to be strong and women to be weak. This balance of weak and strong reestablishes in his mind a natural order to the family and cools the anxieties he may feel about an Oedipal victory—beating out his father. A passive-aggressive man feels he poses no danger to a strong man. The guy, after all, is someone who can absorb his hostility without getting hurt. Knowing that a male authority figure can take his blows lessens the need to test him.

However, other synaptic connections fire when he works for a woman: it contributes to his belief that he, and men in general, are weak and vulnerable. Since he feels easily threatened to begin with, it's too much of a shock to his self-esteem. He needs to prove how strong he is and that nobody can push him around, especially a woman. Resentment and anger inevitably erupt, but never directly—he fears her authority, leading him to channel his hostility toward her passive-aggressively.

THE PASSIVE-AGGRESSIVE ORGANIZATION

It's not only individuals who operate through passive-aggressive moves: organizations, too, can be built upon the tenets of indirection, compromise and conformity. To succeed or even to survive, mastery of passive-aggression is necessary. It's here that I notice the power of passive-aggression. Some men act in an extremely passive-aggressive manner at such companies from nine to five, but show no signs of it in any other area of their lives.

Bureaucracies and institutions (government offices and hospitals, for example) top the list as the most passive-aggressive. They are also, typically, the least efficient organizations because there are few real incentives to work harder or for the common good. Workers tend to think of work as resignation to job/paycheck/insurance coverage/retirement benefits/security and stasis, rather than career commitment/income/perks/golden parachute/security and growth. Those with thwarted ambition tend to slacken off (often under mountains of superfluous paperwork) and expend only halfhearted effort. Consequently, these people are tremendously frustrating to work with, unless you are a complicitous insider or outsider.

It is *thwarted ambition* that most plagues bureaucracies, subtly encouraging passive-aggression. No matter how hard a man works, he can never accomplish enough or be fully recognized for his efforts. His supervisor, a perpetrator of passive-aggression, will see to that. Each individual's contribution is merely a drop in the bucket, so he'll do enough work to accomplish something and meet his supervisor's demands, but not enough to truly succeed. His ambition, decisiveness and drive are drained from him drop by drop by organizational inertia.

If you've worked for a bureaucracy, you probably have found there a character as ubiquitous as the compulsive record-keeper: the "Man Who Does No Wrong." Of course, this senior executive has appointed a number of inept middle managers because he needs to surround himself with unthreatening yes-men. This serves two purposes. No one can rise through the ranks who poses a challenge to his leadership, and secondly, by surrounding himself with incompetents, he has convenient excuses for why things fail when they do. It is never his fault.

Passive-aggressive organizations are easy to identify. Time is wasted in unproductive power struggles between employees who should be cooperative. Workers are more concerned with their circumscribed and selfish agendas than with a universal focus on reaching a goal. Back-stabbing and petty bickering are all too common, too often. Good ideas die a slow and wretched death. Communication is especially confusing— memos are written in a kind of doublespeak where one thing means something else. Messages and true meanings flounder beneath streams of circuitous verbiage and self-conscious diplomacy. Worst of all, you can never tell where someone's loyalty lies. This leads to a gray aura of mistrust.

Passive-aggressive organizations operate with a form of "parallel processing." Here's what I mean. A boss treats his second or third in command passive-aggressively, and then those subordinates treat *their* subordinates the same way. The behavior is handed down through the ranks until it pervades the culture of the entire organization. In such a stultifying and debilitating atmosphere, everyone feels alienated and unhappy, and takes it out on everyone else.

Just as passive-aggression is about how the weak resist authority, the flip side of passive-aggression is how the powerful try to enforce submission. Certain organizations and employers are more authoritarian and therefore foster passive-aggression. Although few of us can change the actual structure of a bureaucracy or get our boss to be less domineering, we *can* affect the clarity of simple daily transactions. A policy of defining clear lines of communication and authority will let people know what is expected of them—and conversely, it will give employees the opportunity to let off steam. This contributes to improved morale, as do incentives to work harder, rewarding assertiveness and productivity and setting common goals.

FINALLY...

Although passive-aggression is common on the job, it is tolerated much less there than it is at home and in social relationships. In the business world where money, property and the survival of others are at stake, an obstructionist is more likely to be shunned, passed over or fired than tolerated. Once a passive-aggressive man breaches a limit, a company tends to be less forgiving than a wife or friend. Screwups are not covered over. At work, relationships can be more impersonal, which makes it easier for colleagues to speak directly to a passive-aggressive man to get him to stop his games and contribute to the larger effort or to get out.

EPILOGUE

IN A CHARMING *New Yorker* magazine humor piece by Polly Frost, the heroine of the story is considering her life, her future and the fiancé who's keeping her waiting outside a movie theater. In a moment of wild clarity (when she knows he's going to stand her up), she admits to herself with resignation that "Jonathan" is just another "*P-A*," that it's her luck to attract passive-aggressive men who "at first, seem perfect" until "the *other behavior* takes over." She remembers a previous boyfriend, a "P-A" named Tim, and her problems with him. She says:

> I had to be the one to decide that it was time for us to take a vacation, where we'd go, how we'd get there. [Tim] waited until we were at the airport to assert himself, just as they were giving the final boarding call. He said he needed to buy a copy of *GQ*, and he wandered off. He never showed up on that flight.

It's both funny and remarkably unsurprising to find a heroine pondering the often imponderable behavior of a passive-aggressive man, and realizing a few truths about him, and herself. Although she's exasperated, she still jokes about the waiting, the delays and the stories a passive-aggressive man concocts to get off the hook. She doesn't spare herself or her *weakness* for this particular brand of modern man either.

Thousands of women like her have paced in frustration, agony or rage, waiting for a passive-aggressive man to come through. Like the tuned-in woman in the story, I hope you're *on to* his machinations. But it's also my hope that reading this book (unlike the story's protagonist) has helped you learn how to protect yourself from passive-aggression.

Throughout, I've spoken in great detail about the feelings and attitudes that comprise passive-aggression. I wanted to help you understand, too, that even though you care about him, you're not responsible for a passive-aggressive man's problems or how he reacts to you. Most of all, I wanted to confirm that you are *not* responsible for getting him to change. While your emotional support is important, getting him to understand his behavior and make changes are the jobs of a therapist.

Also in these pages, I've cleared up a few mysteries about this personality, providing answers to the questions most frequently asked about him:

—*Why* is a man passive-aggressive? The qualities that technically make a man "passive-aggressive" are, for example, denial and disowning of anger; fears of intimacy, dependency and competition; managing conflict with excuses, procrastination and self-sabotage. I tried to show you how he might have become passive-aggressive by examining his early childhood experiences (for example, how his parents might have shaped his character by reinforcing and rewarding certain behaviors and punishing others); I considered the possible influence of social structure and sex roles on shaping his personality and disposition, and how imbalances of power in relationships foster passive-aggression.

—*Who* is the passive-aggressive man? I probed his complex behavior one aspect at a time, examining his tenuous attitudes toward intimacy and sex, how he relates as a husband and father or as a force in the workplace, where he has to test his ability to compete with other men. And, very important . . .

—*What* are you getting out of your relationship with him? Why do you fall for the "P-A" in spite of yourself? I hoped to help you figure out what your modus operandi is around passive-aggressive guys. Do you humor them? Find their evasiveness a challenge? Perhaps you are too much the complement of a passive-aggressive man by being either a Victim (you take your lumps and don't fight back effectively), a Rescuer (you do too much for him, fall for his excuses and mother him) or an implacable Manager (you won't take no for an answer). I tried to paint a clear picture of how you behave, giving you the kind of information you need to figure out your place in the equation.

What I think will help you most is understanding that:

—A passive-aggressive man is responsible for how he feels, no matter how persuasively he denies those feelings rather than accepting them.
—A passive-aggressive man is in charge of the choices he makes, good and bad. *The same is true for you.*
—You must be clear about your expectations in a relationship with a passive-aggressive man, communicate them, enforce whatever limits you set and get out, if necessary.

Unfortunately, understanding alone doesn't bring about change. It takes effort—his and yours.

If you value the relationship—really see promise and potential joy in it—your best tack may be to take a step back and use all your powers of gentle persuasion and affection to get the passive-aggressive man into therapy. There comes a time when you reach the limits of your ability to make change in a relationship, when his personality problems are no longer your responsibility. That's the time when the passive-aggressive man should seek professional help.

I want to end this book on this note because psychotherapy is so important in the scheme of things. Therapy with a passive-aggressive patient who wants to make changes can set in motion a cascade of personality growth that influences how he behaves at home and on the job. With sufficient motivation on his part, understanding his dynamics and expressing concern or love for him on your part, and with a therapist's expertise, I have great hope for the maturity the passive-aggressive man can achieve.

Therapy is not only about recounting one's life in a safe and nonjudgmental setting. It is about probing those events you choose to bring up (or that come up by association) and examining feelings to see how they affect your behavior now. Not all of one's personal history is pleasant and not all feelings are reconcilable. Therapy may open a Pandora's box of life's conflicts, joys and miseries, but as in the legend, opening the box also releases *hope*. Therapy, then, helps clarify who you are and offers a chance to give up behavior that keeps you stuck so that you can start again and get the most from life.

But what gets the passive-aggressive man into the therapist's office? Certainly, you shouldn't hesitate to suggest it gracefully. If his personality problems are causing serious difficulty in either his job, home life, social or family relationships, then therapy is indicated. Neither you nor the passive-aggressive man himself stand to gain by denying problems when they are present, and when they are affecting your lives together. There's nothing heroic about *not* asking for help. If he alone needs therapy, or if the two of you need therapy together, then by all means seek it out. When the personality problems are less serious (or pervasive), then a little fine-tuning in therapy may be beneficial, but I would not consider it "necessary."

It shouldn't be difficult to find the name of a well-recommended therapist. There are several different types of therapy, all of which have been proven effective for passive-aggression: individual "psychodynamic" therapy where the passive-aggressive man can address his fears of intimacy, dependency and competition; specialized "behavior" therapy that helps the patient to become more assertive; and "couples" therapy that focuses on improving communication between the passive-aggressive man and you.

The passive-aggressive man will be unable to benefit from any of these treatments unless and until he is sufficiently motivated, when he's troubled enough by the consequences of his behavior to act: his passive-aggression has gotten out of control, and most likely, his life is out of control. Maybe he was fired from a job he really liked and pinned his hopes on; or he is so anxiety-ridden about his children that he won't let them show any initiative; or his wife finally left him after threatening to do so for several years.

The bottom line is that highly motivated patients make progress. What moves them is the *recognition that a problem exists, and that it has a cost.* Thus begins productive treatment. What doesn't work is to coerce the passive-aggressive man into therapy against his will. The fundamental personality changes he makes must be for himself, not because you or others put pressure on him.

Psychotherapy is an expensive and time-consuming process requiring sustained commitment over the course of months, or even years. But *staying in* is what counts. Mark Twain said in *Pudd'nhead Wilson,* "habit is habit, and not to be flung out the window by any man, but coaxed downstairs a step at a time." Therapy is a lot like that; there is no instantaneous, clean "cure" for personality problems, including passive-aggression in all its complications. It's one step at a time toward self-awareness, even though you may lose your footing and slip a few times. What matters is summoning the energy to keep going and a willingness to make the walk.

Ultimately, in therapy, a passive-aggressive man comes to understand how he can assert himself without being hostile, that he ought not to be afraid of his own aggression, that others aren't out to control him or demand too much of him and that there are ways other than passive-aggression to deal with his frustration. When a passive-aggressive man can stop saying "no" long enough to figure out what his own feelings and wishes are, he can finally emerge as his own man.

To improve the quality of his life—and yours—a passive-aggressive man must begin in therapy to make choices out of a desire to grow up. This means:

—He must be willing to acknowledge what he feels.
—He can free himself from feeling immobilized by the past.
—He must be aware of what he's doing to perpetuate situations that keep him where he is.
—He can gain fulfillment in an intimate relationship, and allow himself mastery at work.

Psychotherapy isn't about removing imperfections of personality, but learning you can control your feelings, understand the repetition of themes ("Why does this always happen to me?"), give up self-defeating behavior and gain self-esteem. Hopefully, with therapy, your boyfriend/spouse/father/brother will take the kind of action that will change his behavior, and then his life and yours.

What the passive-aggressive man learns about himself and what you've learned about him in this book is a guide for both of you—a place to begin mending relationships and clarifying misunderstandings. I think that now you understand the complexity of passive-aggression, and that there is no simple word or deed that would overnight transform a passive-aggressive man into a non–passive-aggressive man. What both of you have is freedom of choice. The passive-aggressive man can choose to remain stuck in denial—and with feelings, attitudes and behavior that never lead to fulfillment—or choose to break out of it. He has capabilities, dreams, goals, a heart, drive—and responsibility to himself to make the most of it all. I hope this book helps him and you in the search for a fulfilled life.

INDEX

ABOUT THE AUTHOR

Scott Wetzler, Ph.D., is a clinical psychologist in private practice in New York, and Associate Professor of Psychiatry at Albert Einstein College of Medicine Montefiore Medical Center. He has published more than seventy-five scholarly papers on various topics in psychiatry as well as several articles for *Self,* the *New York Post* and other general-interest magazines.